ND   Cox, Trenchard,
553   1905-.
F6
C6   Jehan Foucquet,
1972   native of Tours

DATE			

JEHAN FOUCQUET
NATIVE OF TOURS

PLATE I (*see page* 89)
THE TRIAL OF THE DUC D'ALENÇON AT
VENDÔME
Boccace de Munich
Munich: Staatsbibliothek (Cod. Gall. 369)
[*Frontispiece*]

JEHAN FOUCQUET

NATIVE OF TOURS

BY

TRENCHARD COX

BOOKS FOR LIBRARIES PRESS
FREEPORT, NEW YORK

First Published 1931
Reprinted 1972

Library of Congress Cataloging in Publication Data

Cox, Trenchard, 1905–
    Jehan Foucquet, native of Tours.

    Reprint of the 1931 ed.
    Bibliography: p.
    1. Foucquet, Jehan, 1415?–1480?
ND553.F6C6 1972   759.4   72-7072
ISBN 0-8369-6926-X

PRINTED IN THE UNITED STATES OF AMERICA

TO MY MOTHER

in whose company, many years ago at
Chantilly, the wonder of Jehan Foucquet
first flashed upon me.

FOREWORD

THE FICKLENESS of Fortune has never been more in evidence than in the case of the painter who makes the subject of this book. In his day, Jehan Foucquet enjoyed a widespread fame and, at a time when Italy was sipping the nectar of the first Renaissance fruits, he was summoned from Tours to Rome to paint the Pope's portrait.

From the close of the fifteenth century until the middle of the nineteenth, the name of Foucquet sank deeper and deeper into oblivion and, even now, its due has not been paid. In the censure of those who wisely study the history of the arts his name is still great, but to the large numbers of people for whom painting is no source of scholarship but a fountain merely of interest and delight, the name of Jehan Foucquet means little and, indeed, is hardly known. If, therefore, this book is able to increase the radius of Foucquet's reputation, its existence will be fairly justified.

During the preparation of my material, I have been constantly indebted to friends in London and Paris for their assistance and encouragement. Without them, the contents of these pages would probably never have been written and to them I gladly extend my thanks.

T. C.

Cheyne Walk
May 1930—*July* 1931

CONTENTS

ILLUSTRATIONS

NOTE

Foucquet's portrait of 'Etienne Chevalier and his Patron Saint' has recently been transferred from the Kaiser Friedrich Museum to the new Deutsches Museum, Berlin.

JEHAN FOUCQUET
NATIVE OF TOURS

'The gravity and stillness of your youth
The world hath noted, and your name is great
In mouths of wisest censure.'
                              —OTHELLO, II. 3.

PART ONE

THE SCENE

PLATE II (see page 43)
PAGE FROM THE 'BIBLE MORALISÉE'
Paris: Bibliothèque Nationale (MS. 166)
[to face page 3]

CHAPTER ONE

THE SOCIAL SETTING

To begin an essay on the subject of French art with a mention of France in the fifteenth century would seem to many people a direct and ill-omened flight into the face of Providence, for, of all centuries, this one in France is the most despised by those who like to charter the progress of the arts by pinning them down to certain periods. To most people, these hundred years suggest an epoch not of artistic activity, but of intense political crisis when the mind of France was fixed exclusively on setting her house in order and on ridding it of its unwelcome invaders. This period, indeed, is considered as one of painful transition in which the intense, religious art of the Middle Ages was crumbling away before the incoming tide of the Pagan Renaissance, leaving behind it, as a momentary residue, an art which was, at once, drab, realistic, bourgeois and humdrum.

But, in reality, this period spanned by the reigns of Charles V and Charles VIII was not completely sterile and the flow of artistic activity was not stemmed despite the interference of continual misfortunes. Certain provinces, indeed, were never more productive than at this moment and the departments of Provence, Artois, Burgundy and the Languedoc employed an increasing number of artists. It is true that in the first part of the century such regions as Normandy, Orleans and the Touraine were temporarily paralysed by the continued pressure of the Hundred Years' War, but after the conclusion of the treaties they, too, regained their strength and were able to turn, with easy minds, to the pleasures which come with peace. Inasmuch as the century progressed, so did prosperity increase and those artists, who had long been unemployed, were able again to set to work. The reigns of Louis XI and Charles VIII were almost proverbial, in certain quarters, for their well-being, and not only were the working people well paid and contented but also the artists found a plenteous outlet for their talents, as is testified by the wealth of sculpture, tapestry, stained glass, miniature painting and all kinds of *orfèvrerie* which, in spite of much destruction, iconoclastic and otherwise, still remains as our inheritance of a period which many of us now profess to despise.

But, for all its inaccuracy, it is not difficult to see how the prejudice against this period arose, for, indeed, the artistic activities of France in the fifteenth century, though varied and considerable, are gravely defective, since they existed in the face of almost insuperable odds. French art in this most unhappy century differed essentially from the Italian art of the same period in that it lacked unity and continuous progression. In Florence, there was one source for all artistic creation and every production from that source was impregnated with the same definite philosophical code. But in France at this period there was no such centre of philosophy and scholarship, and the seed of artistic production was sown over an immense and far-flung area. In Florence, moreover, art remained entirely native and, therefore, homogeneous, whereas in France, the artists were tossed hither and thither on a turbulent sea of political trouble and their art became infused with extraneous elements. In certain regions, especially on the banks of the Loire and in Provence, Italian artists mingled with the French and the characteristics of French art became changed. At Avignon, the heart of the Papal territory, we find continual impressions of Italian influence, whilst at Angers reigned the Duke of Anjou, René, who was famed for his interests in things foreign and for his absorption of cosmopolitan culture. It cannot, therefore, be a source of astonishment that the French art of this undisciplined period should reflect a philosophy which is as varied as it is perplexing.

But even here, criticism may be too carping and what was lost

by the lack of concise centralization was to a certain extent regained in the abundance and freedom of invention, the spon-
taneity and variety of imagination, and the freshness and gaiety of
observation which this philosophical insouciance produced. In
the fifteenth century, art flourished as an everyday element—a
naïve and popular expression of national thought.

The scene of this present history must necessarily be set in the
Touraine, for it was at Tours about the year 1420 that Jehan Foucquet
first saw the light. Tours in the fifteenth century was by no means
a smug and colourless country town but a city of style and importance, both picturesque and lively. It was, after 1450, a recognized
centre of prosperous commerce and its nearness to Loches and
other royal residences kept it continually in the public eye. It was
the home, also, of various distinguished members of the nobility
and was inhabited by many State dignitaries, both civil and ecclesiastic. Its population, moreover, comprised a large foreign colony
in which both ambassadors and artists were represented. Under
Charles VII, Tours was a flourishing city of no mean nature, but,
with the accession of Louis XI, its style further increased and it
became the seat of the Government and the capital of France.

It is to the information of certain Italians that we owe our
knowledge of the brilliant living which took place in Tours in the
fifteenth century. In 1461, two days before Christmas, the Ambas-
sador of the Florentine Republic arrived in Tours, with a suite of
a hundred persons, to welcome the accession of the new king,
Louis XI. During the three weeks of their visit, Tours was *en fête*.
The magnificent pageant of their official entry into the city was
followed up by an unbroken sequence of official functions, including every variety of reception, concert and sumptuous entertainment. Every detail of this festive Christmas season is given us
in the *Archivio Storico*, which follows up a minute description of
the whole incident with a full list of the by no means frugal expenses. This invaluable document was drawn up by a high State
official—obviously a man of sensibility and distinction—and his
lucid description of the experiences of the ambassadorial mission

reveals to us the existence of a lively social life in Tours, in which an extremely joyous and hospitable society took part. The author of the *Archivio* tells us that one of the heaviest items in the entertainment consisted of the payment and gratuities given to the singers and musicians (players of the lute, zither, harp, trombone, tambourine and all kinds of music) whom the visiting ambassadors and the French nobles enjoined daily to play beneath their windows. Never a night fell or morning broke in Tours unaccompanied by the melody of serenade or aubade. The feasts themselves, indeed, were enlivened by novel and entrancing distractions and the costs of the visit were considerably amplified by the fees paid to singers, dancers, conjurers and reciters of joyful legend.

Another Italian informer on the circumstances of Tours in the fifteenth century to whom we owe our gratitude is Francesco Florio, a cultivated and much travelled gentleman who will again prove our best friend when we have to attack the disheartening problem of the biography of Jehan Foucquet. Florio was a foreigner of exceptional culture; he had explored the most remote parts of the world, including Africa and Asia, and he had lived three years in Paris. After many wanderings in France he arrived in Tours, a city which fitted so exactly the requirements of his scholarship and sensitive intelligence that he chose it as a convenient place in which to pass his final years.

It is to a letter written by Florio, in 1477, to his friend Tarlati, that we have to turn for information. In this piece of friendly correspondence, Florio plunges into a long and laudatory description of the city in which he had decided to live. He praises its delicious climate, its warm winters and perfect summers. He allows, moreover, a special word of adulation to the water of the Touraine, which, he insists, can outrival that of Rome in its purity and health-giving qualities. 'No purer water seeks to break through its pipes in the suburbs of Rome than that which, here in the Touraine, rushes down the well-ordered water-courses, and bubbles on the banks.' The abundant harvests and the gracious

6

PLATE III (*see page* 49)
PORTRAIT OF CHARLES VII
Paris: Musée du Louvre
[*to face page* 6]

Touraine wines delight him and he remarks that here Ceres reigns with Bacchus in perfect harmony. The wines, he says, neither clog the blood with their heaviness nor dry the taste with their acidity. The fruits, too, win Florio's meed of praise; he deems them fit for the Hesperides' garden and he notes, particularly, a kind of pear called 'Le Bon Chrétien', praising it for its hardiness in growing and its peculiar excellence of flavour.

Francesco Florio as a gourmet was unashamed, but his taste for pleasure did not end with the table and his interest in art was great. He was a sincere, broad-minded and eclectic art lover with a touch of that unbounded and insatiable curiosity which marks the true lover of life, with all it has to offer of novelty and variety. He was an intense admirer of Tours' architectural beauty, with its undulating girdle of gilded ramparts and castellated turrets; its towers, steeples, narrow streets and coloured roofs; its many churches and palatial dwellings. He rhapsodizes over the Cathedral, calling it 'a beautiful church, joyous and faultless, and so well proportioned in all its parts that the mere sight of it, from within or without, turns sorrow into happiness and sadness into joy'—a praise which surely would have surprised even Maistres Papin and Dammartin, the learned but modest architects of this unpretentious edifice.

Florio was a fairly constant attendant at the Cathedral services, but he went even more frequently to the Basilica of St. Martin, which he considered as architecturally more edifying than St. Peter's in Rome and where he spoke of the clergy with an awe and admiration which would not have been unfitting to the Pope and all his Cardinals. He adds, moreover, that the piety of the priests in Tours is especially impressive and should be a shameful reproach to certain of the Roman clergy, particularly those of the Church of St. Paul beyond the Walls where the insolent priests left their duties to the care of monks who were as incompetent as they were unwilling.

Florio praises, too, the music of both these principal churches in Tours, but he declares that the finest music of all is to be heard in the Chapel Royal of the Old Castle near the Loire, where each day Mass and Vespers are sung by the royal choir—a perfectly trained assembly of boy singers under the direction of a certain Jehan van Ockegham,[1] the choirmaster and keeper of the Treasure, a man of surpassing grace of body and mind. Florio states that Ockegham was a learned musician and an inspiring teacher who could instil into his pupils such excellence and truth of song that they were a living testament of the power which the human voice can hold over all instruments of music. Music, indeed, seems to have played an important part in the life of the average Tourangeau and it is not surprising that songsters and choir-boys make frequent appearances in the work of that arch-Tourangeau, Jehan Foucquet.

Florio used to delight in taking long walks and it is not extravagant to suppose that he was on occasion accompanied by Foucquet. Sometimes, in the cool of the evening, he would choose to wander past the Chapel Royal and walk down to the river until he came to a broad stone bridge of recent construction. Here he would find a path which would lead him to the Abbey of Marmoutier, where he had access to the many valuable volumes in the Abbey library. At other times, he would prefer to leave the city by the West gate and to make his way to the home of some wealthy bourgeois family—perhaps the Le Plessis or the family of the Montils—where he would find some pleasant company and fair exchange of talk. It is certain that Florio moved in the highest social circles that Tours had to offer, and he could, when necessary, be equally at his ease with gentlemen of fashion, sharing their sport with the falcon or at the chase, as he was in converse with the learned Canons of the Basilica of St. Martin.

Florio's enthusiasm included a firm liking for all the inhabitants of Tours. He admired the *belle santé* of the French and especially

---

[1]According to Monsieur Georges Lafenestre, Ockegham was the friend of Foucquet and also, perhaps, the friend of Hans Memling. He is known to have been at Bruges in 1484, on the occasion of a musical competition, and to have been royally entertained by the artists of that city.

PLATE IV (see page 50)
PORTRAIT OF JOUVENEL DES URSINS
Paris: Musée du Louvre
[to face page 8]

of the Tourangeaux: he observed, too, that they lived to a good, healthy old age, particularly as compared with the Italians, who rapidly became wrinkled, ill and uncontrolled in body and mind. The politeness of the French people seemed to Florio to equal its reputation and he could not speak too highly of the women, whom he considered noble, refined, modest and beautifully gowned. His friends were mostly made in learned circles and the majority of his evenings were passed in quiet talk with the Canon of Saint Gatien, a man 'as godly in manners as he was sound in scholarship'. Florio, in short, lived a life of such happiness at Tours that he never contemplated returning to his native land; he confided in Tarlati that never again would he be induced to leave this place of final refuge where he had found a healthy and luxuriant country inhabited by people who seemed to him entirely charming. It is, however, not too extravagant to surmise that Tarlati was astonished by his friend's decision, for none loved the arts better than Florio and none was more fully aware than he that Florence at that time was the soil in which the finest flower of Italian art was sown and was the home of artists of whom he himself had expressed admiration, such as Gozzoli and Lippo Lippi, della Robbia and Donatello.

But Tours, itself, was not devoid of artistic society, for in addition to Foucquet and his pupil, Michel Colombe, both of whom were influential *maîtres d'atelier*, there was a highly esteemed confraternity of artists, comprising such famous folk as Mathurin Poyet and his son (the latter one day to become the court painter of Anne of Brittany), Pierre André, painter to Monseigneur of Orleans, Coppin Delft, favourite of King René, and Jehan Perréal, famed as sculptor, painter, decorator and architect, who had come from Lyon to Tours to draw the cartoons for the great rose-window in the Cathedral.

There was, indeed, a great demand for art in Tours at this time and magnificent examples of the architect's skill were springing up along the banks of the Loire. The rich commercial, ecclesiastical and diplomatic communities of Tours encouraged artistic production, and employed sculptors, goldsmiths, tapestry weavers and all kinds of craftsmen to heighten the elegance of their houses. Tours was, in fact, a city where feasting was the rule and, in many months of the year, there was an unbroken sequence of sumptuous celebrations. The men and women of Tours, indeed, did not allow time to weigh heavy on their hands and they indulged in a splendid programme of balls, processions, concerts and plays.

This, then, is the *milieu*, grave and gay, in which we are to find our artist, Jehan Foucquet. Foucquet, in his miniatures, will make all the elements of this many-coloured city live again for us in colours more vivid than those which the most ardent words of the Italian traveller could paint. In the mirror of his art, we shall see reflections of every facet of the city's life. We shall observe its cosmopolitan society; its ecclesiastics, captains and financiers; its diplomats, scholars and men-at-arms. We shall scan the faces of the homely crowd; the rustic population of labourers, sailors, fishermen and market folk. We shall be led along the tortuous alleys of the city, where we catch an occasional glimpse of the homes of the rich with their stately interiors and sumptuous carpets. We shall be taken, too, past more modest houses of red and black brick and roofs of slate, until we find ourselves outside the city walls, wrapt in enjoyment of a spacious panorama of blue hills and fresh green fields cut into winding patterns by the spiral waters of the river Loire.

CHAPTER TWO

THE INTELLECTUAL BACKGROUND

ALTHOUGH THE flower of intellectual culture is of a nature so fine that the faintest disturbance would seem sufficient to blow it away, the root from which it springs must be inversely hardy and immune to Fortune's most ill-intentioned strokes. It has been seen that not even a series of wars which embraced the span of an entire century was able to kill the growth of this sturdy French plant and, in circumstances which would appear destructive to any form of intellectual progress, culture continued as best it might. But the Hundred Years' War could not fail to have an effect of devastation and only the most persistent spirits were able to maintain their stand. It seemed at the beginning of the fifteenth century that the war had evaporated all scholarship; the Universities had difficulty in keeping open and the scholars were dispersed. Industry, too, seemed at a standstill and we are told that, in 1436, the municipal council of Orleans was unable to find a master builder or a body of workmen capable of re-constructing the city's bridge, which had been partly destroyed in the siege of 1428-9. The critical state of France at this time caused alarm in learned circles as well as among the politicians and we have record of a distressful letter written by the Archbishop of Bordeaux in which he says, 'Those who are disposed to seek the pearl of science can no longer take refuge in the Universities and many who have found their way there have been imprisoned, robbed of their books and belongings, set to ransom, and sometimes, *O douleur*, have been put to death'.

Beneath the oppression of this unspeakable misery, the life of the intellect could not fail to dwindle, but it never reached extinction.

The first half of the reign of Charles VII was not entirely devoid of cultural development and, at the end of the reign, both art and letters burst forth into a rapid efflorescence. The years which produced such men as Villon, Foucquet and Antoine de La Sale can hardly be called sterile, and later, in 1473, the field of literature was to be embellished by the birth of another distinguished writer, Jean Lemaire de Belges, who was subsequently to praise in poetry the artists of France, including our modest denizen of Tours, and to become the chief apologist of what is now considered one of the darkest of the centuries.

This persistence of intellectual life is a phenomenon for which it is difficult to account and it is best to regard it in the light of a relic left by the preceding century: an epoch in which a universal curiosity had been awakened and the achievements of philosophers and artists were given their due respect. In the fourteenth century, the nobles extended their patronage to learning and the fine arts, and their protection was given to theologians, historians, poets, painters and artists of all kinds. This influence persisted even in the restless days of the fifteenth century and various members of the court and the nobility vied for excellence in the rôle of Mecaenas.

Among those in high circles who looked favourably upon the arts was no less a person than the King himself. Charles VII, for all his eccentricities and deprivations, was a man of culture and an enthusiast for the arts. His tastes, it is true, concerned literature rather than painting and he was a genuine lover of books. His critical faculty was sound enough to permit him to acknowledge Chastellain as a great historian and a fine Latin scholar, and it was his expressed wish to select as counsellors men who were learned in matters scientific as well as political and ecclesiastical.

Next to the King in importance as a stimulating force in the encouragement of learning and the fine arts came the Duke of Burgundy, Philip the Good. This prince, by reason of his ownership of land in the Low Countries, was one of the wealthiest nobles in Christendom and his taste for luxury and feasting was in pro-

PLATE V (*see page* 51)
ETIENNE CHEVALIER WITH HIS PATRON SAINT
Left panel of the Diptych of Melun
Berlin: Kaiser Friedrich Museum
[*between pages* 12 *and* 13]
[N.B.—*This picture has recently been transferred to the new
Deutsches Museum, Berlin*]

PLATE VI (*see page* 52)
THE VIRGIN AND CHILD WITH ANGELS
Right panel of the Diptych of Melun
Antwerp: Musée Royal des Beaux-Arts
[*between pages* 12 *and* 13]

portionate scale to his riches. Life for him was a perpetual gala and his existence was ennobled by all the splendours art could give. Being a poet himself of no mean qualities, Philip's favours were especially directed to those who shared with him the mastery of the Poetic Muse, but his tastes were eclectic rather than specialised and he spent his money liberally as well as wisely. Enormous sums were spent by him in the interest of art and letters, and no expense was spared in the purchase of works of art and in the organization of magnificent pageants and theatrical displays. As a bibliophile Philip was unrivalled and his spacious library contained many precious books and was noted for its display of handsome bindings. He maintained a posse of illuminators and calligraphers always in his service, as well as a number of translators and scholars, all learned in special subjects. To Philip, Duke of Burgundy, all the authors of France looked with reverence and affection and he was regarded throughout his life as the arch protector—indeed, almost as the patron Saint—of literature and of the art of printing, then in its growing pains and badly in need of support.

Another, and hardly less important, patron of the arts was René, Duke of Anjou and Lorraine, Count of Provence, and King *in partibus* of the Two Sicilies. René did not enjoy the full cycle of Fortune's wheel in the manner of Philip of Burgundy, nor did he possess such riches as were the lot of that happy prince. Politics had never gone well with René and both his dukedom of Anjou and his County of Provence were ruined by the Hundred Years' War. But his private tastes were neither coarsened nor embittered by his public worries and he remained throughout his life a man of refined and quick intelligence and insatiable curiosity. René's ruling passion was for the accompaniments of culture and he extended his favours to all facets of the intellect.

From 1443-1471, René resided principally in Anjou: he employed architects to add to his already sumptuously appointed castle and he took pleasure in laying out gardens of appropriate magnificence. René was a man of cosmopolitan tastes, and he prided himself as a fancier of rare flowers, exotic plants and strange animals. His court, however, was not among the most extravagant, but was elegant and original. As a centre of culture, it was almost unrivalled; musicians, actors, artists, scholars, alchemists, astrologers and all men of science crowded there and received due welcome.

René's taste for good living and the more exquisite pleasures of life was not entirely fortuitous, since he inherited much of the intellectual and bibliophilic qualities of his uncle, the Duc de Berry. His interest, moreover, in artistic matters did not end with mere patronage, and René, himself, could wield the brush and pen. His literary works were well known among contemporary readers and ranged from didactic or allegorical works in prose or poetry to a treatise on Christian morals. The lighter side, too, was not neglected and he was the author of *Regnauld et Jeanneton*, a pastoral, as well as of several *Cantiques* and *Rondeaux*. These works are not mere exercises in literature, but a real expression of the author's tastes, in which his passion for the arts of literature and chivalry is duly reflected. They reveal, moreover, René's love of country life; in the pastoral he speaks ecstatically of the pleasure gained by watching peasants at their work, and he mentions the names of four bulls in the royal stud: Brunet, Blanchet, Blondeau and Compagnon.

Of René's paintings we know little, as no trace of them remains, and it is doubtful whether the loss to art is great. He, himself, expressed no pride in his pictorial efforts, although we know that he was ambitious enough to paint an *Image* of the Crucifixion for the Franciscan brothers of Laval.

A less important patron of the arts, although the only one to secure immortal fame by his own literary productions, was Charles d'Orléans. It is as a poet that Charles d'Orléans is now remembered, but in his life he was considered as a protagonist in the encouragement of the Muses. Most of his later life, after his captivity, was spent at Blois in modest and peaceful retirement, during which time he compared himself to an old cat, drowsily sleeping away his final years. At times, Charles was so poor that he wore clothes which were pieced together, but he always managed to maintain an atmosphere of intellectual plenty. What he saved on his wardrobe, Charles spent upon his library and he possessed many precious books. His interest in poetry was unbounded and he inaugurated the practice of setting poetic competitions among his satellites. His attendants, moreover, were mostly men of intellect, although not always of exceptional talent. His favourable reception of poets at Blois was well known, although out of all who assembled there most were mediocre and only one, François Villon, was great.

Amongst other artistic patrons, one could mention such persons as the Comte de Dunois, Eleanor of Bourbon, Etienne Chevalier, Jacques Cœur and Gilles de Rais, the last of whom combined his literary inclinations with activities so extraordinary that his patronage of artists has since been eclipsed by the fame of his perversions and sadistic practices.

It is, perhaps, significant to observe that the element of culture was not, at this time, entirely confined to the wealthier classes, since there are many evidences that the people themselves were far from insensible to the pleasures of the intellect. Whenever a theatrical performance was in progress, the crowd flocked to see it, and at times the standard of entertainment was high. In many towns, literary societies were organized by the younger members of the bourgeoisie, who, although they did not entirely eschew certain convivial pleasures, took the discussion of literature as the object of their meeting. In the North, small bourgeois academies (*les Chambres de Rhétorique*) were formed, in which an exceedingly abstruse and pretentious versification was practised.

But in spite of all these traces of learned and artistic impetus, and of a desire for learning which, willy-nilly, persisted in making itself felt, the intellectual life of the fifteenth century was deficient and the generation which arose under Charles VII was badly educated. As has been already observed, the progress of art and letters in France at this time was local rather than general and the chain of knowledge had been broken. The continued political crisis had destroyed the sense of unity and solid support, and the spirit of culture, though existing, was more or less fortuitous. In certain circles, the desire for learning was great, but many notable people were still sadly ignorant. One of the King's counsellors, Jehan de Lannoy, confessed that he never went to school, and felt ashamed in the Council Chamber before all the learned clerks and eloquent lawyers and dared only agree with everything that had been said. 'Maistre Jehan ou Maistre Pierre a bien dit' was all he had either the courage or the knowledge to exclaim!

It was certainly not the people's fault that ignorance, at this period, was rife, for there was a very evident desire to learn in various parts of France. Even amid the most troublous times, Universities were founded; the Universities of Caen and Poitiers saw the light in 1432, whilst that of Bordeaux came into being in 1441. In 1432, moreover, the Pope, Eugene IV, accorded to the University of Angers Chairs in Theology, Medicine and the Fine Arts, all of which faculties had before been lacking. In most parts of France, the schools were prosperous and well patronized and many of the small parochial or municipal institutions were success-ful. We have particular knowledge of the prosperity of schools at Chartres, Rouen, Troyes and Valence. In Paris, the Université de Navarre achieved success, and a new independent college, that of Sainte Barbe, was inaugurated.

But in spite of the will to learn, the results were arid and the methods of teaching were abominable. The theologians and men of learning remained completely mediaeval; their methods were out of date, their productions decadent, and their philosophical formulæ often very feeble. The learning in the schools and col-leges was stereotyped and unprogressive; nothing new was taught. Doggerel (*glossa cacabilis*) was spoken instead of Latin and the treasures of ancient Hellas were yet entirely undiscovered. Philosophy was regarded as the key to knowledge, but the standard of thought was negligible and the Faculty of Philosophy

PLATE VII (*see page* 55)
PORTRAIT OF A MAN
Vienna: Liechtenstein Gallery
[*to face page* 17]

in the time of Charles VII had no professor whose name is worthy of mention.

This general feebleness of instruction induced a terrible decadence in the Church as well as in the Universities. The University of Paris, for example, was in the hands of Maistre Thomas de Courcelles, a pernicious charlatan, who had been one of the judges in the trial of Joan, although he later denied the charge of ever having been present at the Court of Rouen. De Courcelles enjoyed a high position in court circles and was enjoined to give the sermon at the last Mass and burial of Charles VII.

Another case of brazen hypocrisy was that of Maistre Fernand de Cordoue, a young Spaniard and member of the University of Paris, who declared that his knowledge was infallible and could confound that of all the doctors at the Sorbonne. When that solemn body commanded him to appear before them to prove his declaration, Fernand de Cordoue prudently refused to be interrogated and left the capital.

In spite of serious reforms, such as that attempted in 1452 by Cardinal d'Estouteville, the standard of learning remained low throughout the century and the students, however willing, found it difficult to reap benefits from their teachers. But wherever there is a desire to learn, there must also be a certain element of success and there were, doubtless, a few independent spirits who had sufficient strength and reason to pierce the aura of stupidity which pervaded the Universities and who could emerge on the other side, free to receive the light of true knowledge and reason unimpaired.

The two principal faculties in the University curriculum were those of Theology and Medicine. It has been seen that the methods of theological instruction were antiquated in the extreme, but they were up to date as compared with the régime of medical teaching. Medicine, in the fifteenth century, was very primitive and practically the only known methods of healing were bleeding and purging, and even these could be extremely dangerous; epidemics followed closely on each other's heels and there was no sense of public hygiene. The private individual had a fairly sound idea of cleanliness and baths were frequently used, but nothing was done by public bodies to secure the health of their municipalities. The state of the towns was filthy beyond conception, and when Louis XI expressed an intention of visiting Angers, three carters were employed for four months to clean the streets. The larger the cities, the greater was the risk of infection and ravages of leprosy and bubonic plague were the order of the day.

Inasmuch as it was useless for people of sense to rely on public bodies for the care of their health, so was it impossible for profound students to rely for instruction upon the seats of learning. The best intellectual life, indeed, existed outside the Church and Universities and, among private individuals, a certain intellectual and scientific progression existed. Astronomers, alchemists and men of science were by no means rare, and geographers attracted attention by their descriptions of foreign lands. It is evident that interest was taken in scientific or exotic novelties, for we know that laboratories, menageries and botanical gardens were instituted in various parts. Interest was also taken in travel, and travellers made careful notes and published them. Guillebert de Lannoy published a history of his voyages in Europe, Egypt, Syria and Palestine, and Bertrandon de la Broquière gives a most interesting account of his wanderings in Syria and the Balkans, making exact notation of climates, customs and racial characteristics. The latter book has left us with a valuable impression of the attitude of an educated man of the late Middle Ages to those who lived in foreign parts, and it is, perhaps, significant that de la Broquière, speaking of the Turks and comparing them with his countrymen, praised them for their generosity and their kindness towards the poor. 'Ils sont moult charitables gens les ungs aux autres et gens de bonne foy. J'ai veu souvent quand nous mengions que, s'il passait un pauvre homme aupres d'eux, ilz le faisoient me~gier avec nous, ce que nous ne ferions pas!'

PLATE VIII (*sse page* 56)
SELF-PORTRAIT
Enamel Medallion
Paris: Musée du Louvre
[*to face page* 18]

CHAPTER THREE

THE LINK WITH LITERATURE AND THE OTHER ARTS

THE FIRST view of the arts in fifteenth century France is a depressing one and the literary landscape at once seems barren. In the art of writing, the worst elements in the fourteenth century had persisted into the fifteenth, and literary agility had given place to an advanced form of mental acrobatics. Endless moralizations, abstruse allegories and an absurdly complicated method of prosody were the fashion, and eloquence had become confused with rhetoric. But even among this morass of muddled intellects, a few isolated geniuses survived and those who had any sense of poetic expression struck a new field of thought. A feeling of sadness and of the futility of life then crept into poetry, and a poignant phase of thought arose, which found its epitome in François Villon, the father of the modern lyric.

In the reign of Charles VII, the writing of poetry was a fashionable diversion and not only the nobles indulged in the making of rhymes, but their servants, grooms and stable-boys followed suit. Even the clerks wrote verses, some of which expressed the sentiment of love but others were merely prompted by such trivial circumstances as a friend's indisposition or the sight of a runaway horse.

Of the amateur poets, by far the most famous was Charles d'Orléans, and his works have since become a classic in French literature. The poetry of this modest nobleman is infused with such a marvellous gaiety and inspired by such an exquisite sentiment of youth and love that its fame can scarcely be a source of wonder. But in form, the poetry of Charles d'Orléans is mediaeval and in spirit it is so light that it seldom surpasses the limits of an after-dinner entertainment. The tragedy of life is excluded from this verse, and, although the author had been taken prisoner at Agincourt and had been held in captivity for twenty-five years, not a vestige of this time of suffering is reflected in his work. In the lifetime of Charles d'Orléans, poetry was considered as a fashionable and agreeable diversion and was regarded with the same kind of superficiality as the theatre is to-day by the tired business man.

Another poet who insisted on excluding the note of serious-ness from poetry was Alain Chartier, a banal soulless rhymester who was regarded by his contemporaries as the greatest poet of his time. Chartier's mind was not entirely vapid, but he reserved all serious thoughts for prose and conformed to the taste of the time by writing trivial love lyrics, which were correct in form but tedious in expression and obscure in thought. His *Bréviaire des Nobles* was dull and didactic but it was claimed as a masterpiece by all serious readers and enjoyed an immense popularity.

Immeasurably the greatest French poet in the fifteenth century was François Villon, a member of the Paris University, but as un-conventional in methods and as mountebankish in manners as that Academy was conservative. In the poetry of Villon, a real note of sorrow is struck and the miseries of the Hundred Years' War here find their due reflection. His entire writings are per-vaded by a sense of brutal disillusionment, and almost every line gives indication of Villon's horror of old age, his fear of death, and of his regret for passing youth. The poems of Villon were the first to utter real despair and with him was expressed, for the first time, a true cynicism for accepted values and a profound sym-pathy for all those to whom life had offered its most squalid aspect.

The language of Villon's verse was essentially popular and was recognized as being the essential idiom of 'les bons becs de Paris'; in the *Testaments* and in the *Ballade des Pendus* a real popular feeling was crystallized and his expression, though understanding of human suffering, contains elements of pitiless mockery and bitter resentment. Villon's poetry, moreover, created a genuine and exclusive taste for the lyric form and dealt the death-blow to the epic; the *chansons de geste* were no more read, and, if they were, their prosody had been so much mutilated as to be unrecognizable or their contents were served up, entirely afresh, in the form of short prose tales of psychological interest, such as the famous collection of the *Cent Nouvelles Nouvelles* and that touching little treatise on conjugal love, *Les Quinze Joyes du Mariage*, may typify.

The dominant taste in the more popular facets of fifteenth century French literature is one of unremitting realism and nowhere is that sentiment more definitely expressed than in the theatre, which developed and thrived upon the desire of the public to find in its entertainment a reflection of the gravity and gaiety of everyday life.

In the fourteenth century, the theatre had existed in a very primitive form, being then entirely undivorced from the trammels of the Church; practically the only dramatic performances were those given outside the church porch, known as the *Miracles de Notre Dame*. With the advent of the new century, the taste for theatrical performances had been more really developed, and the simple *Miracles* had turned into elaborate *Mystères* to which the whole municipality flocked and which continued in favour for well over a hundred years, until they were forbidden by law of the Paris Parliament. The attraction of the *Mystères* was manifold and it must be admitted that the scenic effects, which at times were undoubtedly magnificent, played an equal, if not greater, part than the play itself. But there were among the large répertoire of mystery plays some in which a real literary element existed, and those who were sensitive to dramatic values could hardly have failed to be moved by the more realistic scenes in such a masterly play as the *Mystère de la Passion* by Arnoul Gréban. Along with the *Mystères* were played, on different occasions, the *Moralités*, shorter plays of less elaborate setting but equally edifying in intention. Some of these *Moralités* were ambitious in design and one, the *Moralité du bien et du mal Advisé*, comprised a cast of fifty-seven personages.

Neither the Mysteries nor the Moralities were completely serious, and the pranks played by such characters as devils and demons (particularly in the *Mystères*) used to make the people rock with laughter. But the aim of these plays was to heighten strictly the moral level and the comic patches were only incidental. There existed, however, in the fifteenth century a facet of the theatre which was purely frivolous and such entertainments as the *monologues*, *soties* and *farces* were intended only to amuse. The humour of most of these pieces was either gross or slap-stick, and they did not usually explore more novel ground for their subject-matter than the stupidity of husbands and the machinations of mothers-in-law.

Very few of these farces appeal to us to-day for any reasons except the merely historical, but there was one, the *Farce de Maistre Pierre Pathelin*, which has remained a classic of French dramatic writing and which, for its humour, cynicism and sense of true comedy, is almost fit to rank with the universal comic creations of Aristophanes and Molière.

In setting the scene of intellectual influences in which Jehan Foucquet found himself, it is important not to be too parochial and it is essential to extend our glances beyond the boundaries of France. The Unity of Place is indeed impossible in stage directions such as these. In the development of French art in the fifteenth century, certain foreign countries played an important part, and chief among them were Italy and Flanders.

In the reign of Charles VII, the knowledge of the artistic miracles which were being performed in Florence was beginning to percolate into France. At the time of the accession of this unhappy King, the full wonder of the Renaissance was dawning upon Italy, and Florence was the centre to which all eyes were turning. In 1422, the year of Charles's accession, Brunelleschi was in middle age and about to begin his work on the sacristy of San Lorenzo; Donatello had begun to startle the Florentines with some of his early masterpieces, and Ghiberti's carving of the door of the Baptistry was nearing completion. In painting, no fewer marvels were

PLATE IX (see page 63)
THE ANNUNCIATION
Hours of Diane de Croy (School of Foucquet)
Sheffield: Ruskin Art Museum

PLATE X (see page 64)
THE ANNUNCIATION
Hours in collection of A. Chester Beatty, Esq.
London

PLATE XI (see page 64)
THE VISITATION
Hours in collection of A. Chester Beatty, E
London

[to face page 23]

being brought to light. Masaccio had just completed his short but peerless existence ; Pisanello, Fra Filippo Lippi, Fra Angelico and all the company of Florentine artists were entering upon their prime. It was, therefore, impossible that France should not feel something from this wave of art which was rolling over Italy, and the influence it had was great. Both René of Anjou and Charles d'Orléans had travelled beyond the Alps and their voyages had made their due effect. Political events, moreover, contrived to make the link between France and Italy more certain and there was a continual exchange between the two countries of merchants, diplomats and artists.

But the influence of Italian art on the French intellect was nothing as compared with that of Flanders, within whose boundaries lay the property of the princely Duc de Bourgogne. Flanders, was the magnet of all Northern commerce and the almost unrivalled centre of European plutocracy. Inasmuch as Italian art was classical, so was the art of Flanders naturalistic, and, instead of deriving its inspiration from the idealistic creations of Greece and Rome, it found its medium in the homely incidents of everyday ·life. The school of painting of which the brothers Van Eyck were the originators was nothing if not domestic and its significance was to have a marked effect upon the painters of France.

It needs, indeed, a distinction which is almost problematic in its nicety to separate the intrinsic qualities of France and Flanders at this time, for the two countries were closely linked together. The Italians, even, were completely confused in the matter of the arts and insisted upon considering Jan van Eyck as French and on calling him 'Johannes Gallicus'. The Flemish were, indeed, continually kept in contact with French thought through the medium of their intellectual leader, the Duc de Bourgogne. The double influence, indeed, of France and Flanders was in a state of incessant counter-filtration, and even such a decidedly national artist as Jehan Foucquet of Tours was not free from the Flemish imprint.

The influence of foreign countries was far more dominant in painting than in the other arts, and in architecture, French artists remained completely unperturbed by the new phase of thought which was sweeping over Italy. The sculpture and architecture of France in the fifteenth century were unashamedly Gothic, and, despite the label of 'flamboyant' which is usually attributed to the buildings which grew up under Charles VII, both these arts remained true to the national tradition.

Among the most beloved of the arts in the fifteenth century was that of music, and we have evidence that the King and wealthy nobles such as the Duc de Bourgogne and Gilles de Rais employed choirs of proportionate magnificence to the adornments of their private chapels. There was, moreover, no public function or festivity which was unaccompanied by orchestral music, and we hear of musical guilds among the laity of certain municipalities. These secular orchestras were small in size and unambitious in their choice of music and they confined themselves generally to the playing of popular melodies on instruments such as the lute, harp, flute, trumpet, horn, drum and portable organ. But religious music, such as was sung in cathedrals and in the chapels of the nobility, was of a more elaborate nature, and it was here that the sciences of fugue and counterpoint first came into their full development.

The fifteenth century produced one musician of lasting reputation, Jehan van Ockegham, a Fleming by birth but a Frenchman by naturalization, who owed his success to the favour of three French kings, Charles VII, Louis XI, and Charles VIII. Ockegham, who has already been mentioned in connection with Francesco Florio, enjoyed the post of 'choirmaster to the King' for more than forty years and his music was well known throughout France for its sweet melody and masterly counterpoint. Ockegham seems to have been a prolific artist and it is said that he wrote, amongst much else, twenty Masses, as many songs, and eight motets of which one was scored for thirty-six separate vocal parts.

The somewhat disconnected contents of the three chapters which form the first part of this book will find their justification if they show that, in spite of the devastation of the Hundred

PLATE XII (see page 63)
THE VISITATION
Hours of Diane de Croy (School of Foucquet)
Sheffield: Ruskin Art Museum
[to face page 24]

PLATE XIII (see page 63)
A FUNERAL PROCESSION
Hours of Diane de Croy (School of Foucquet)
Sheffield: Ruskin Art Museum
[to face page 24]

Years' War and of the paralysis, both commercial and artistic, in certain regions of France, the arts were not completely killed. Even in the full flood of disorder, the brilliance had not gone out of art and letters, and Jehan Foucquet, the most magnificent French painter of the Middle Ages and one of the most marvellous of all time, was to follow closely on the heels of the greatest period of unhappiness. This persistence of the artistic stimulus in a period of such exceptional misery is, indeed, a phenomenon at which to wonder and is a striking proof of that unquenchable vitality which has always been regarded as a quality supremely French.

PLATE XIV (see page 64)
A FUNERAL PROCESSION
Hours of Cardinal Charles de Bourbon
Copenhagen: Kgl. Bibliothek

[to face page 27]

PART TWO

THE ARTIST

CHAPTER FOUR

THE MYSTERY OF HIS LIFE

THE CIRCUMSTANCES of Jehan Foucquet's youth and the facts of his entire life are still partially shrouded in mystery and much patient research has revealed only a few rare landmarks in his biography.

There are, however, two cardinal points of which we can be certain: one is the information given us by Robertet in his note at the end of the *Antiquités Judaïques* stating that the illuminations were begun by the *enlumineur* of the Duc de Berry and continued 'by the hand of the most excellent painter and illuminator of King Louis XI, Jehan Foucquet, native of Tours'; and the other is that during the pontificate of Pope Eugene IV, Foucquet was summoned to Rome, to paint the Pope's portrait.

Apart from this knowledge that our painter was under royal patronage and that he received the honour of a welcome at the Vatican, all the information which we possess about Foucquet's life is incidental, and much of it is trivial. But in all the references to the artist, the meed of praise is high, and the fact that he has sunk from the pinnacle of reputation to the merest outskirts of oblivion is only another testimony to Fortune's vacillating favour. In his day, Foucquet enjoyed an awe-inspiring reputation and few chronicles of the fifteenth and sixteenth centuries omit his name. It is, indeed, in the survey of these contemporary—or nearly contemporary—writings that our only hope lies of assessing some of the incidents of the artist's life; and, although the material with which they provide us is nothing more than mere *olla podrida*, it is of incalculable value to anyone whose patience allows him to fit the jig-saw pieces of evidence into a connected pattern.

Of the various references to this native of Tours, none is scathing and most are expressed in terms of praise. In 1495, a member of the court of Charles VIII, in describing the royal estate of Poggio Reale near Naples, says 'this house of pleasure is more delicious than the fair speech of Maistre Alain Chartier could tell, than the subtlety of Maistre Jehan de Meung could write, than the hand of Foucquet could depict in paint'.

In 1503-4, Jean Lemaire de Belges makes two mentions of our artist. In the *Plainte du Désiré ou la Déploration du Trépas de Monseigneur Loys de Luxembourg*, Lemaire sets such artists as Leonardo, Gentile Bellini and Perugino in the same rank as more ancient masters such as:

> *Marmion jadis de Valenciennes*
> *ou (que) Foucquet qui tant eut gloires siennes.*

To the list of ancient artists, he appends Poyet,[1] Rogier van der Weyden, Hugues de Gand,[2] and Joannes Memlinc 'qui tant fut élégant'.

In his more celebrated and more ambitious poem, the *Couronne Margaritique*, Lemaire de Belges tabulates a list of painters who deserve their fame, including Jehan de Bruges,[3] 'le roy des peintres', van der Goes, Bouts, Marmion, Memlinc and Colin d'Amiens; but the two first, he insists, are Rogier van der Weyden and Jehan Foucquet of Tours.

> *(Car) l'un d'iceulx estoit maistre Roger*
> *L'autre Foucquet, en qui tout los s'emploie.*

Jean Lemaire's judgment upon artists may seem a little unbalanced, but his interest in the arts was great and his knowledge of Foucquet was by no means haphazard, since his protectress, Marguerite of Austria, possessed a little Madonna by the artist. In the inventory of the possessions of this royal and cultivated lady is inscribed a description of 'un petit tableau de Nostre Dame, bien vieulx, de la main de Foucquet, ayant estuy et couverture'.

---

[1] Esteemed fifteenth century miniaturist employed by Anne de Bretagne for the decoration of a Book of Hours.

[2] Hugo van der Goes.   [3] Van Eyck.

PLATE XV (see page 67)
ST. JOHN AT PATMOS
Hours of Etienne Chevalier
Chantilly: Musée Condé
[to face page 30]

Another significant reference to the esteem in which our Tour-angeau was held is given by Pèlerin le Viateur, in the third edition of his treatise, *De Artificiali Perspectua* (1521). Here he quotes Foucquet as among the finest decorative painters of France, Germany and Italy,—in fact, of Europe,—and he ranks as his peers Mantegna, Perugino, Leonardo, Raphael and Michelangelo.

But it is not only among his compatriots that we have to look for enthusiasm, since the name of Foucquet was known in Italy as well as France and he found a place in the writings of various Italian chroniclers. In an architectural treatise written by Filarète, a Florentine sculptor and architect who had worked in the service of the Duke of Milan and at the Vatican during the period of Foucquet's residence in Rome, there is a discussion of painters suitable to decorate an Ideal City. Filarète here deplores, in the interests of this Utopia, the early deaths of Fra Angelico, Domenico Veneziano, Pesellino and Castagno, and he informs the Duke that he will have to wait until the dearth of great artists in Italy is relieved. But, he exhorts, the ducal impatience can be satisfied if Monsieur will only search abroad, for there artists are to be found. 'You must see, my lord, if in foreign countries artists are to be discovered; at one time there was one of the highest excellence, Jehan de Bruges, but he, alas, is also dead. I am told, however, that in the Low Countries there is another master, Rogier by name, whose gifts are great, and that in France there is a certain Jehan Foucquet.[1] If he is still alive, he is a fine master, especially in the art of creating life-like portraits. He has painted, in Rome, the Pope Eugene attended by two members of his family and the likenesses are such that they seem Life itself. He has painted them upon a canvas which has since been placed in the sacristy of the Minerva. I mention them because he made the portrait within our living memory.'

For an even more laudatory expression of Foucquet's greatness we have again to turn to that ecstatic letter to Tarlati from Francesco Florio. In his important letter to his friend in Rome, Florio

[1]Filarète calls him Gradetto or Grachetto.

sings the praises of Jehan Foucquet above all other artists, and he speaks in rhapsodies of the wall paintings by Foucquet in the Church of Notre Dame la Riche. Florio's opinion of Foucquet is almost fanatical, and he considers him to be the finest painter of religious subjects who ever lived. His rhetoric knows no bounds. He defies antiquity to boast of Polygnotus, or to extol Apelles. 'For me', he cries, 'I would be happy if I could find words worthy to celebrate the paintings of this master of the City of Tours. Pray do not think I am romancing. . . . Look for yourself at the speaking likeness of the Pope in the Church of the Minerva. . . . Do not doubt that I am speaking the truth when I tell you that this Foucquet can create a living likeness and could rival even Prometheus himself.'

It is one of the great calamities of artistic history that both the wall paintings in Notre Dame la Riche and the Papal portrait in the Roman church have disappeared, for their quality bears all the evidence of having been equal to their fame. Both the Italian texts, quoted above, praise the likeness of Eugene, and the reputation of the portrait lingered on into the sixteenth century. There is a mention of it even in Vasari, who includes remarks on Foucquet in both the editions of his work. In the first edition of the 'Lives', Vasari states that Foucquet's (whom he calls Giovanni Fochetta) arrival in Rome on the Papal Commission coincided with the death of Simone, the brother of Donatello, and that the Pope's portrait was considered a work of high excellence and received the praise of Filarète, with whom the artist was closely associated.[1] In his second edition, Vasari slightly amplifies the statement and declares that 'a little time after the death of Simone, Filarète returned to Rome and died at the age of 69, his body being buried in the church of the Minerva, where, during his period of papal service, he had made arrangements for Foucquet to paint the likeness of the Pope'.

[1]'Capito in questo tempo a Roma Giovanni Fochetta, assai celebrato pittore, che fece nella Minerva il Papa Eugenio, tenuto in quel tempo cosa bellissima; et dimesticosi assai con Antonio [Filarète].'

PLATE XVI (see page 67)
THE ADORATION OF THE MAGI
Hours of Etienne Chevalier
Chantilly: Musée Condé
[*to face page 33*]

Pope Eugene IV died on the 23rd February, 1447; therefore, Foucquet's commission must have been realized some time before this date, and Filarète's papal service must have been of a contemporary period. But in the first edition, Vasari adds that the association of Foucquet with Filarète came to an abrupt and tragic end, since, as the result of a supper which the two artists had together in the country near Rome, Filarète was seized with a fatal attack of dysentery. Filarète's death took place in 1469 or 1470 and for Foucquet to have been present at that disastrous meal would have implied a second journey to Italy, some twenty years after his summons to the Church of the Minerva. Such a theory is not entirely inadmissible but it is unlikely. One thing is certain, and that is that Foucquet did not remain in Italy from the time of Eugene's death to the day of Filarète's contraction of dysentery, since we have evidence that he was in France between the years 1447 and 1470. Even Vasari, however, is reticent of the theory of the second Italian journey, and after the first edition, he lets the subject drop. The second printing of the 'Lives' was more circumspect than the first and Vasari's conscience may have compelled him to omit the story of Foucquet's fatal last evening with his Florentine friend.

Perhaps the most important of all references to the artist is that found in the *Antiquités Judaïques*, the precious book which was once in the possession of the second Duc Pierre de Bourbon, whose secretary, François Robertet, between the years 1488 and 1503, inscribed therein that the greater part of the miniatures were the work of the 'bon paintre et enlumineur du roy, Louis XI, Jehan Foucquet, natif de Tours' (cp. Pl. XXXVI). Although Robertet's statement may seem a little dry after the transports of Francesco Florio, his inscription in the Manuscript is an exceptional phenomenon and of the very highest significance. Such a laudatory inscription as this written by anyone other than the artist was extremely unusual and is a proof of Foucquet's great reputation and of the admiration in which he was held by Robertet.

A later connection with our artist is given us in the mention of

1556 by Jehan Brèche, a lawyer of Tours, who, in one of his legal treatises, mentions Foucquet and his two sons. But his remarks are no complimentary reflection of his taste since he places the whole Foucquet family, including Maistre Jehan, as artists, well below Jehan Poyet.[1]

With this disparaging reference, the curtain comes down upon the history of Foucquet and an interval of over two centuries elapses before we hear his name again. The long silence was, at last, broken in 1739 by the Abbé Jourdain, in a *Mémoire Historique sur la Bibliothèque du Roy*, but the remarks contained in this treatise do not greatly broaden the radius of our knowledge. The Abbé has relied entirely upon Robertet for his information and mentions merely that under Louis XI there was an illuminator, named Jehan Foucquet of Tours, whose skill especially revealed itself in the embellishment of the *Antiquités Judaïques*.

With those remarks there comes another long interval, and we hear no more of Foucquet until the nineteenth century, when, in 1818, M. Chalmel, an historian of Tours, gives a place to the artist in his *Tablette Chronologique de l'histoire civile et ecclésiastique de Touraine*. Chalmel's knowledge is a little wider than that of the Abbé Jourdain and he is acquainted with the observations of Francesco Florio as well as with Robertet's note. His sense of scholarship, moreover, is considerable, and he sets the execution of the Papal portrait to the date of 1443.

The ball of Foucquet's regained reputation was now set rolling and in 1834 that versatile being, M. Crespy-le-Prince, who combined the activities of squadron-leader, painter and art-critic, wrote a short tale called *La Fille de Fouquet*[2] which was conceived in the romantic style and bore many reflections of the art of Sir Walter Scott, and especially of the novel *Quentin Durward*. This short account achieved a fine success, and it brought the name of Foucquet

---

[1] Inter pictores, Johannes Fouquettus atque ejusdem filii Ludoicus et Franciscus. Quorum temporibus fuit et Johannes Poyettus, Fouquettiis ipsis longe sublimior optices et picturae scientia.

[2] Published in a periodical, *France et Italie* (Nov. 1834).

into the public eye. But as a work of scholarship, the writing of Crespy-le-Prince is of doubtful value, since it is peppered with absurd and puerile anachronisms. In one portion of his story, for instance, two persons of the court of Louis XI are—most precociously—overheard conversing upon the subject of Ossian! But there are passages contained in the tale which are of great importance and Crespy-le-Prince has evidently traced the connection of Foucquet with Jehan Robertet, 'greffier de l'Ordre de Saint Michel' (the father of the annotator of the *Antiquités Judaïques*), and he refers to the Robertet family as being great friends of Foucquet and his household.

Crespy-le-Prince did not gain all his information through his own personal research, but drew upon his friend and companion, Comte Auguste de Bastard d'Etang, for much of his knowledge. Bastard d'Etang was a passionate bibliophile and a fine scholar, and in his colossal work *Les Peintures et Ornements des Manuscrits*, he was the first of the later scholars to give Foucquet his due recognition. His enthusiasm for our artist was so great that at one time he intended to publish, in reproduction, Foucquet's complete works (as far as they were then known), and when this proposition proved too costly, he expressed the wish to publish, in colour, the *Antiquités Judaïques*. His appreciation of Foucquet was intelligent and his judgment was sufficiently sure to allow him to esteem the artist as 'a worthy forerunner of Leonardo, Dürer, Holbein and Raphael'.

Both Crespy-le-Prince and his friend Bastard d'Etang set Foucquet in fashion and only a very short time elapsed before a whole constellation of scholars and critics clustered around him. Waagen, Laborde, Curmer and Lafenestre all extolled his worth and attracted the public's attention towards the artist. Justice, therefore, had at last been done and Foucquet was, after many years, duly chartered among the celebrated painters of the world's history.

The contents of this chapter must already have been sufficient to show that it is only with a few pieces of evidence, mostly very uncertain and all of them widely scattered, that we have to fit together the pattern of Foucquet's life. It is, therefore, an intricate and discouraging task to attempt to form any continuous biographical design, and, in any such attempt, we are compelled to return, for our basic evidence, to the annotator of the *Jewish Antiquities*.

François Robertet tells us two things, both of which are certainties. The first is that Foucquet was a great court painter, and the second that he was a native of Tours.

Although there is no doubt that Foucquet was of Tourangeau origin and was born in Tours, we know absolutely nothing of his childhood and upbringing; a complete silence enshrouds his early life and the first activity in which we hear of him engaged was the painting of the Papal portrait.

Many opinions have been formed around the date of Foucquet's journey to Rome; Chalmel considered that Florio's letter indicated that Foucquet was in the early twenties at the time, and that the portrait was painted about the years 1442 to 1443. This would fix the date of Foucquet's birth to the region of 1420.

It is evident that Foucquet remained some time in Rome, and we know that it was in the Eternal City that he met his friend, Filarète. It seems certain, too, that the artist was young at the time, for Florio speaks of Foucquet's journey to Italy as occurring whilst he was still a young man (*in ipsa adhuc juventa existens*).

Chalmel's dating of the portrait of Eugene IV is a possible hypothesis but is open to doubt, and Anatole de Montaiglon, in his *Jehan Foucquet et son Portrait du Pape Eugene IV*, challenged Chalmel's opinion by dating it somewhat later and by expressing the opinion that the portrait was completed any time between 1443 and 1447.[1]

---

[1] Pope Eugene was exiled from Rome in July 1434 and did not return until September 1442. He died on 23rd February 1447. It is, therefore, a sound hypothesis to suppose that Foucquet was in Rome sometime after the Pope's return, since it is extremely unlikely that the portrait was painted during the Pope's exile (1434-42).

PLATE XVI

THE VIRGIN AN

CHEVALIER AN

Tours e

Chant

[betwe

VIII (*see page* 67)
LD WITH ETIENNE
S PATRON SAINT
e Chevalier
ée Condé
6 *and* 37]

Of Foucquet's sojourn in Italy we know nothing, and we have no evidence of the length of his visit, nor of the date of his return to France. According to the present stage of scholarship, fourteen years elapse before we hear of him again and this time it is in connection with a no less lordly personage than the King of France himself. Charles VII of France died at Bourges on 22nd July, 1461, and tradition demanded that an effigy of the dead King should at once be made. The death-mask was taken and cast by a sculptor, Pierre de Hennes (or Hannes), who, according to the ancient evidence of an archive, repaired from Bourges to Paris 'où il pensait trouver Foucquet, le peintre'. This reference, therefore, indicates that Foucquet's commissions in France did not keep him confined to Tours but took him, northward, to Paris.

But his stay in the North cannot have been for long, for in the autumn of the same year, 1461, all Tours was agog at the prospect of the state entry of the new King, Louis XI, into the city and Foucquet was engaged to direct activities. A great daïs was to be erected for the King's reception and Foucquet was consulted as to how it should be decorated. After many vacillations, he took the decision to make it a royal blue, and to have embroidered in the centre a huge golden sun bearing the royal arms. A counter-pattern of the 'Couronne', in white and red, was to be scattered over the blue ground and the entire canopy was to be embellished with a rich golden fringe and angels were to besport themselves in each of the four corners.

The arrival of the King was to exceed the mere formalities of a state procession and the event was to be made the excuse for feasting and carnival. Theatrical displays of the most elaborate order were arranged and preparations were made for the production of mysteries and farces. Three master-artists were employed for the festival: the sculptor, Pierre de Hennes; the architect, Simon Chonain; and the painter, Jehan Foucquet.

But at the last moment, when the city's excitement was at its crest and every preparation had been made and even the scaffolding had been erected for the procession, a royal edict burst like a thunderclap upon the city announcing that the King found displeasure in all forms of elaborate celebrations and that the welcome of the citizens of Tours must be more in accordance with his tenets of economy, both personal and public. The whole scheme, therefore, was rejected and Tours was disappointed.

Louis XI was a man of severe disposition, hard and unimaginative, and his programme was one of strict frugality. When consulted at Amboise as to whether he would enjoy these 'fainctes et mistères faiz en chazands', he replied curtly: 'Non, je n'y prend nul plaisir'. And that, being a royal pronouncement, finished the matter. All Foucquet's work was, therefore, wasted, but he received, with his colleagues, 100 *sols tournois* as indemnity for his labour and wasted time.

Foucquet, however, was to receive many favours from the King, and throughout his life he enjoyed royal favour. In 1469, Louis XI instituted a new Order, the 'Ordre des Chevaliers de Saint Michel', and the statutes of this order were luxuriously drawn up in the form of a magnificent book, of which the frontispiece was painted by Foucquet.[1] There was, moreover, a series of pictures painted by Foucquet for the Order but unfortunately none of them remains, nor is there any precise account of their quality or appearance. There is only the simple statement of André Briçonnet, in an inventory of the royal expenses, that Jehan Foucquet received payment for certain pictures painted for the Order of Saint Michel.[2]

From now onward, the references to Foucquet become more scattered and less significant. During the same year, 1469, we read of him taking part in a general meeting at Tours of the 'bourgeois de la ville'. In 1472, he left Tours for Blois, where he was

[1] Now in the Bibliothèque Nationale, Paris (MS. fr. 19819).

[2] 'A Jehan Foucquet, peintre, la somme de LV livres tournois pour XL escuz d'or, laquelle le roy nostredit seigneur lui a ordonné et fait bailler comptant, le XXVIe jour dudict mois de décembre, sur ce qu'il luy pourra estre deu pour la façon de certains tableaux que ledit seigneur lui a chargez faire pour servir aux chevaliers de l'Ordre de Saint-Michel, nouvellement prinse par iceluy seigneur pour ceci . . . L.V.lt.'

commissioned to illuminate a Book of Hours for Marie de Clèves, duchesse d'Orléans and widow of Charles d'Orléans, the poet. The injunction ran as follows: 'de faire certaines histoires, tourneure et enlumineure d'or et d'azur en unes Heures'. The painting of this book did not take long, and in July of the same year the book was finished and the Duchess awarded the painter 110 *sols tournois*.

According to one document, said to have been discovered in the collection of Benjamin Fillon, Foucquet, just before Pentecost in 1474, painted and gilded another Book of Hours for Philippe de Commines, the historian, for which he received twenty-three crowns, the first instalment of thirteen crowns being paid on the 23rd May, 1474, and the remainder later on. But the doubts as to the authenticity of this reference are great and it is not even certain whether the document ever existed. Foucquet's connection with Commines is, therefore, more unreliable than the merest hearsay and has been rejected by all the most recent scholars.

Another false report, at one time fully believed, asserts that Foucquet executed a Book of Hours for Jehan Moreau, 'valet de chambre de Louis XI' and a fellow-native of Tours. But this suggestion has most sweepingly been rejected, since it is undoubtedly the result of a misdirection and is a variation upon the theme of Foucquet's connection with Commines and refers to the same manuscript.

In 1474, Foucquet again appears to have been working for the King, this time with the solemn task of designing the royal tomb. Louis XI in his lifetime was much preoccupied by the edifice which was to commemorate his place of burial and he ordered that the monument should be erected by three celebrated artists, Michel Colombe, Colin d'Amiens and Jehan Foucquet. A record of the year 1474 tells us that Colombe made a little model, cut in stone, to test the King's approval and that Foucquet received twenty-two *livres* for having drawn up a cartoon of the proposed design.

This last and rather mournful reference is the ultimate important landmark in our tracing out of Jehan Foucquet's career. In 1475, we know that he entered definitely the royal household and could affix to his name the title of 'peintre du roy'. In the next year, 1476, he made a daïs (this time without frustration) for the solemn entry into Tours of the King of Portugal, Alfonso V, for which task he was granted twelve *livres tournois*. In 1477, we have the letter of Francesco Florio in which Foucquet is hailed with such a paean of praise, and in 1481 we have the evidence that he is dead. In an account, drawn up on the 8th November of that year by the Chamberlain of the College of Saint Martin at Tours for the bursar of the same college, there is a mention of 'la veuve et heritiers de feu Jehan Foucquet, peintre'. Jehan Foucquet, painter and native of Tours, had, therefore, probably met his death sometime in the preceding year.

The artist left two sons, Louis and François, and both of them were painters, but their talents were probably mediocre. The lawyer, Brèche, mentions them in his *livre de droit*, but without enthusiasm, and the lack of knowledge on this subject is no great loss. It is possible that a letter written in 1473 by the author Robert Gaguin mentioning a certain 'Egregius pictor Franciscus' refers to François, but the idea is pure hypothesis and Gaguin's high expression of esteem is certainly contradictory to Jehan Brèche's barren comments.

The general impression left by this, perforce, disconnected review of Foucquet's life is one of great success. Foucquet, indeed, enjoyed no brief Saint Martin's Summer of fame but gained a lasting and widespread reputation, although no record exists of his death being celebrated by any special mark of respect. He seems, in fact, to have died in complete simplicity as an *homme de métier* and a humble citizen of Tours. But practically throughout the whole of his career, Foucquet was concerned with royal and highly spectacular persons. In his youth he was employed at the Vatican; he was, also, given encouragement by Charles VII, whose portrait he painted.

PLATE XIX (*see page* 68)
THE ANNUNCIATION
Hours of Etienne Chevalier

Under Louis XI the patronage of royalty was made even more certain and he became a member of the Household.

He painted, too, for the nobility as well as for the court. Robertet's famous note reveals that Foucquet executed most of the miniatures in the first volume of the *Antiquités Judaïques* for the great collector and connoisseur, Jacques d'Armagnac; and this note comprises the extra significance of fixing the date of the decoration of this portion of the manuscript to some time before 1476, since in that year its owner became a political prisoner in the Bastille on the charge of high treason and was put to death in the following year, as a pernicious and dangerous rebel.

There is, moreover, reason to believe that Foucquet received commissions from many celebrated personages. The portrait of Jouvenel des Ursins in the Louvre seems almost certain to be by Foucquet and the rôle played in the artist's life by Etienne Chevalier, the King's favoured financier and counsellor, is continually reflected in his work. In this connection there appears one extraordinary *lacuna* in the biographical evidence, since no mention of Chevalier's name is to be found. Yet he must, indeed, have been one of Foucquet's most important patrons, since the famous Hours at Chantilly are directly due to him. There is also a portrait of Etienne Chevalier in Berlin which, like the Chantilly Hours, is almost indubitably by Foucquet although unauthenticated by documentary proof. It must not, however, be thought that the part played by the King's counsellor was the greatest influence in Foucquet's life, since the more recent researches of scholars— and particularly those of Comte Durrieu—have proved that this view is a mistaken one.

CHAPTER FIVE

THE PROBLEM OF THE JUVENILIA

THE NINETEENTH century critics, to whom the first researches upon Foucquet are due, were not content merely to
sun themselves in the light of their new discovery, but soon
found that the 'bon paintre et enlumineur du roi Louis XI'
was as controversial as he was excellent. They became aware,
indeed, that, with each new discovery of his work, the question
of a date must arise and that their argument must continually
revolve around the Italian journey.

The common agreement is that Jehan Foucquet went to Rome
between the years 1443-47, and that, at that time, his fame was
sufficiently great to cause the Pope to desire a portrait from his
hand. The mystery, therefore, of his youthful activities immediately presents itself, and the first thought which springs to the
mind is of Foucquet's *juvenilia*. 'What was his talent before he
left for Italy? Did Foucquet have an early manner? If so, which of
his surviving works are a mirror of this time?' These, indeed,
were the questions which everyone was asking, and, unfortunately, they are asking still.

The problem of our artist's *jeunesse* has never been properly
solved and there are still many dark shadows into which light has
refused to penetrate. One thing, however, is certain: the clue to
our searchings for examples of Foucquet's youth must be found
in works which reveal traces of that unimpeachable quality of the
mature artist tempered by the clumsiness which can only be the
result of a young man's inexperience.

Of the larger works of Foucquet which have been thought to
have been painted before the great event of his journey, the only

existing example to which such an hypothesis has been attached is the 'Portrait of Charles VII' in the Louvre which some consider to have been the cause of the Pope's commission. The usual and most likely date given for this picture is 1454, but certain scholars who support the theory of the earlier date claim that Foucquet's portrait reveals the King as a man younger than fifty, and maintain, with a lesser degree of capriciousness, that the style is too simple and completely mediaeval to be that of a man who had recently been to Italy and absorbed its full influence. The question of the King's age is a matter of visual opinion but the background against which he is placed is, certainly, plain enough and has none of the Italianate richness which can be seen in its companion piece, the portrait of Jouvenel des Ursins. But with these two points of stylistic conjecture the matter must end, and those who claim that the skill with which Foucquet portrayed the French King was the cause of the Papal favour must indeed be allowing their enthusiasm for discovering examples of Foucquet's *juvenilia* to blind their eyes to the light of obvious facts. The portrait, indeed, is unlikely to be a very early work and, as will be seen in the next chapter, it reveals many traces of a date later than Foucquet's pre-Italian years.

The two protagonists in the fight for the rights of our artist as a young man are M. Victor Bouchot and the Comte Paul Durrieu.

M. Bouchot, in the *Gazette des Beaux Arts*, attributed to Foucquet's pre-Italian period some pages, each decorated with eight miniatures, of a *Bible Moralisée* in the Bibliothèque Nationale (MS. fr. 166). As is usual when new ground is explored, M. Bouchot's statements were at once contested and a new field of controversy was opened. Immediately, the critic became the target for the keenest shafts of contestation and few who studied Foucquet's work could do more than admit that certain qualities (of colour and style and landscape background) in these little miniatures were reminiscent of the master, though they did not, in any way, stand as a proof of his early activity (Plate II).

Bouchot, however, persisted in his choice of argument,

ascribing the miniatures to the period of Foucquet's life when he was 'encore tâtonnant, non point débarrassé franchement du Gothique enseigné à l'atelier des anciens'.

His colleagues, however, refused to follow him thus far, maintaining that the miniatures were too amateurish even for the master's youth and were by some unknown master belonging evidently to the same *milieu* as Jehan Foucquet, but quite distinct from the artist to whom we owe the miniatures at Chantilly and the *Antiquités Judaïques*.

Both these phases of opinion have met with their supporters, and the question is still hanging in the balance. M. Bouchot was first reminded, in these leaves, of Jehan Foucquet by the predominance of the *type tourangeau*, by the sparkling qualities of the colour, by a strong architectural interest, by the frequent representation of a river winding its course through a fresh and airy landscape under an azure sky, and by the general similarity of the landscape to the country round Tours. This similarity of style and atmosphere to Foucquet's work is, indeed, undeniable and extremely provocative of conjecture, but it can hardly be considered as definitive evidence of Foucquet's direct authorship, since the distinction between the work of Foucquet himself before he was in full possession of his talent and that of a skilled master of the same school is so subtle as to be uncertain and even indiscernible.

M. Bouchot's article, however, with its stimulating hypotheses, provided a spring-board from which progressive minds could once more dive into the limitless ocean of discovery, and one of the first to elaborate his theory was the Comte Durrieu.[1]

Comte Durrieu, after years of deep research, arrived at the opinion that there are at least four manuscripts which contain miniatures by the same hand as those in the *Bible Moralisée*. It will, perhaps, be as well to classify them in the order in which the critic quotes them.

First, the *Mer des Histoires*,[2] a Latin manuscript in the Biblio-

[1] *Bulletin de la Soc. Nat. des Antiquaires de France*, 1804-1904.
[2] *Bib. Nat. MS. Lat.* 4915.

thèque Nationale, said, by M. Léopold Delisle, to have been executed for a member of the family of Jouvenel des Ursins, and, perhaps, for the great *chancelier* himself. The book contains miniatures by diverse hands, but a strain of Foucquet can at times be seen.

Secondly, the *Thésaide* or *Amours de l'Architecte de Palémon* in the State Library at Vienna (MS. 2617). This manuscript was, perhaps, commissioned by René d'Anjou, the famous patron of the arts.

Thirdly, Comte Durrieu quotes the copy of the *Stratagèmes*[1] of Frontin in the Royal Library at Brussels, and fourthly, he exemplifies the Boccaccio *Des Cas des Nobles Hommes et Femmes Malheureux* in the Library at Geneva (MS. fr. 191).

The last two manuscripts, although at first sight they seem far removed from the kind of work which up to now we have associated with Jehan Foucquet, have a special significance and merit a more expansive elaboration.

The manuscript of the *Stratagèmes* in the Brussels Library recalls René d'Anjou even more emphatically than does the Vienna *Thésaide*. The unknown translator of the *Stratagèmes* has dedicated the book to Charles VII, King of France, and states, in the prologue to the Sovereign, that he was commissioned by 'aucuns de messeigneurs vos familiers'. At the head of the manuscript, moreover, is a little miniature representing 'The Presentation of the Book to Charles VII'. In this painting, of very minute proportions, the King is represented sitting in an armchair, whilst, next to him, there stands another King, crowned, and wrapped in a blazoned mantle, which, thanks to the brilliant preservation of the pigments, reveals certain heraldic details which pin the wearer's identity down to King René of Anjou. The significance of this fact is great, since it shows that King René must, in some way, have taken a personal part in the circumstances which led to the execution of the Brussels *Stratagèmes*.

The origins of the fourth manuscript, the Boccaccio at Geneva, are unknown, but each of the nine large miniatures which herald

[1]MS. 10474.

the various sections of the book is reminiscent of the Vienna *Thésaide*. It is, therefore, especially curious that two manuscripts out of these four should reveal so strong a connection with the King of Anjou, and it seems that there is one startling conclusion which can be drawn from this phenomenal evidence: that our mysterious master of the *Bible Moralisée* and its kindred manuscripts worked for René and had once been counted among the company of the 'peintres du roy de Sicile'.

If, then, it could be proved that this master was the young Foucquet, the result would be of enormous importance, since it would mean that Foucquet, as a youth, had served in René's court. Another corner of the veil which shrouds this part of our artist's life would thus miraculously be lifted.

Here, M. Durrieu elaborates his thesis further, and finds more food for speculation in the various minute portraits (six in number) which the artist of the Brussels manuscript has encircled in the *lettres historiées*.

These six portraits are, indubitably, by the same hand as that of the miniature of the 'Presentation', and all of them, both in style and technique, are masterpieces of the most scrupulous precision. They reveal, also, a phenomenal breadth of modelling which makes us at once rack our brains to find a parallel and which recalls most strongly the frontispiece of the 'Status de l'Ordre de St. Michel', a work which is almost incontestably by Foucquet.

The portraits represent various classes of people; the first three depict a peasant and two young people, all of whom appear to be of a distinctly Tourangeau type; the fourth is a portrait of a young ecclesiastic, which reminds one of the figure of St. Nicholas in the Hours at Chantilly; the fifth reveals a portrait of a young clerk whose face bears an expression of sad resignation, immediately recalling the figure of St. Stephen in the panel at Berlin, and the sixth represents a young man of an unusual type, much akin to that of the famous portrait in the Liechtenstein Gallery at Vienna and to the young man of the famous enamel medallion in the Galerie d'Apollon at the Louvre, which is said to be a self-portrait

of none other than our great Jehan Foucquet. There is undoubtedly a difference of age in the portrait of the Brussels Frontin and
the self-portrait of the Louvre medallion, but the type remains the
same. The eyebrows and the line of the nose, the hollow chin and
thick lips can easily be traced in both the portraits. The two faces,
indeed, even though they might not be identical, are sufficiently
alike to be the faces of two near relations.

It is not, then, so very fantastic to suppose that these portraits
are by Jehan Foucquet, since we have evidence that, in early youth,
the artist excelled in portraiture. Filarète speaks highly of this
facet of Foucquet's accomplishment and praises his portraits 'quoi-
que ce soient des œuvres de la jeunesse du peintre'.

Comte Durrieu's comparison of the Brussels manuscript with
Foucquet's work does not end here, although he does not in any
way expound his theory as something incontestable. He merely
states it as a reasonable and fascinating suggestion. In addition to
the portraits, he remarks that in the background of some of the
miniatures there are figures painted in gold-like metal, very reminiscent of those statues or statuesque figures which occur so
frequently in the Chantilly Book of Hours.

The net result, therefore, of Comte Durrieu's discussion is not
in any way conclusive or doctrinaire. He traces, with considerable show of reason and much scholarly ingenuity, the connection between the author of the manuscript at Brussels and René
d'Anjou; he suggests, moreover, that the best portions of the
book, namely the miniature of the 'Presentation to the King' and
the six small portraits, are by Jehan Foucquet, and he claims that
the likelihood of Foucquet's authorship of the four books mentioned, as well as the *Bible Moralisée*, is by no means so remote
as some might readily suppose.[1]

[1]Other manuscripts which Comte Durrieu quotes as possibly the work of
Foucquet's youth are:
Manuscript of Tourangeau origin (Liturgical use of Nantes) (British
Museum, addit. MS. 28785).
'Livre des Anges.' Geneva (MS. fr. 5).
'Chronique Universelle' (Bibliothèque Nationale, MS. fr. 15445).

CHAPTER SIX

THE QUESTION OF HIS PORTRAITS AND ENAMELS

W E ARE already sufficiently acquainted with the facts of
Foucquet's life to realize that as an artist he was complete,
and as a painter he was entirely accomplished. Both in his private
and public capacity, he was a man of many parts and was versatile
enough to fit himself for every facet of artistic activity. Much of
his work has not survived and, for the excellence which he must
have shown in his mural paintings, altarpieces, tapestry, cartoons
and other things, we can only take as evidence the words of his
contemporaries and the praise of certain friends. All we possess
of Foucquet's work is lamentably little; much rests upon supposition and only one manuscript among his entire œuvre is definitely authenticated. Two enamels, a drawing or so, about a
hundred miniatures and a mere half-dozen portrait pieces complete the sum of our possession. We have, in fact, only a handful
of evidence on which to appraise this celebrated and prolific
painter, but we may feel, on the other hand, some consolation in
that, whereas of Foucquet something has remained, of the work of
his contemporaries we have nothing. Of painters so highly
esteemed as Pierre de Hennes, Jacob de Litement and Coppin
Delft not a trace remains, and of the renowned Jehan Perréal[1]
and Jehan de Bourdichon we have only the faintest echoes.

Foucquet's friends and contemporaries were united in acclaim-
ing him as the most excellent of portrait painters, and it was in
this phase of painting that he won the highest praise. Unfortunately, the portrait of Pope Eugene is lost, but we have a certain

[1]Perhaps identifiable with the Maître de Moulins (of whom a masterpiece
hangs in the National Gallery).

PLATE XXII (*see page* 70)
THE CORONATION OF THE VIRGIN
Hours of Etienne Chevalier
Chantilly: Musée Condé
[*to face page* 49]

PLATE XXX
THE CORONATION OF THE VIRGIN
Hugo d. Spanish School
Chantilly: Musée Condé
See for page 103

idea of what it must have been. We know that it was a large—perhaps, even, life-size—composition, representing the Pope attended by two dignitaries of the Vatican. Our knowledge, moreover, is furthered by the existence of an engraving (in the Bibliothèque Nationale) of the principal figure of the composition. Even through this inadequate medium certain of the qualities which made the portrait famous appear, and the print reveals a gravity and accuracy of presentation, a simple nobility of design, and a scrupulous attention to nature and detail.

Of the five discovered panels, all of which may, with reason, be attributed to Foucquet and which have portraiture as their main interest, two are in the Louvre, one is in Berlin, one is at Antwerp and another is in Vienna. Of the two panels in the Louvre, the more interesting, although the less spectacular, is the portrait of Charles VII (Plate III). This picture, as has already been indicated, is regarded by some scholars as an example of Foucquet's early talent, such as it was manifest before the journey to Rome. This point of view does, indeed, at first seem attractive, and a glance, first at this picture and then at the portrait of Jouvenel des Ursins on the same wall, is superficially reassuring, since it can at once be seen that the portrait of Charles reflects no trace of Italian influence, whereas the flamboyant background of the portrait of the Chancellor is a flagrant advertisement of Foucquet's predilection for Italianate decoration. One cannot, at first, easily imagine that the background of the King's portrait, with its two little green curtains, primly parted, represents the work of a receptive genius who had just returned from Italy, his mind ablaze with the glory of the *Quattrocento*. But, interesting as it would be to assign the portrait to Foucquet's pre-Italian years, it would not be reasonable to do so since the balance of evidence in almost all respects tips against the theory's favour. The portrait of Charles, indeed, bears a significant inscription in the words 'le très victorieux roy de France'. This title was never used of Charles VII until after the taking of La Guyenne, and, if the inscription were genuinely added by the artist, it would date the panel to a year not earlier

than 1451—long after the limit of Foucquet's sojourn in Rome—
and would place the King's age to the fifties, which would by no
means be unreasonable.

The modest mien in which the King is presented would, then,
be only another tribute to Foucquet's sense of characterization and
historical detail, for Charles VII, despite his recognition of the
title 'très victorieux', was, even after the triumphs of 1451, plunged
in a mood of pitiable melancholy, and his public successes only
resulted in intensifying his private disillusionment. Agnès Sorel,
the fair, was dead; the Dauphin, in exile, was a continual menace,
and the King felt himself enmeshed in a network of treason and
conspiracy. He presented, indeed, a bizarre and unhappy figure;
the victim of crushing sorrows and bitter regrets. Foucquet, a sensitive psychologist, did not fail to observe the royal mood, and
in the Louvre portrait he represents the King, meagre, sorrowful
and down-at-heel, hearing Mass between the windows of his box
at the Sainte Chapelle at Bourges—the very edifice in which the
picture remained until the building was destroyed in 1757 by the
orders of the Cardinal de la Rochefoucauld.

This portrait is not unique among likenesses of Charles VII,
for Foucquet portrayed the King again in the miniature of the
'Adoration of the Magi' in the Book of Hours of Etienne Chevalier (cp. Plate XVI). Here we may see the King, still grotesque and
serious but in a more noble circumstance, kneeling before the
Virgin, and in a mood less sad. The subtle difference between the
two portraits is an impressive proof of Foucquet's keen appreciation
of character and swift observation of the vagaries of human
temperament.

The second portrait in the Louvre, that of Jouvenel des Ursins
(Plate IV), is a more vigorous achievement, and represents the
painter at a more mature stage of his development. Here the
background is a joyous riot of gilding, in which Corinthian
columns surmounted by escutcheoned capitals clearly tell the
tale of Foucquet's Italian experience. The portrait of this ample
Chancellor, contented to a degree which is almost Rabelaisian,

PLATE XXIII (*see page* 70)
THE ARREST OF JESUS AT GETHSEMANE
Hours of Etienne Chevalier
Chantilly: Musée Condé
[*to face page* 50]

makes a striking contrast with its companion portrait of the un-happy, emaciated King. The Chancellor's clothes are as rich as the King's are dowdy, and he wears a magnificent fur mantle, with a golden purse hanging from the girdle. The high import-ance of this personage is everywhere emphasized, and at once we recognize the sitter as a man of power and persistence, who rose from the humble origin of a draper's son to be a puissant dignitary of State, rich, solemn and magisterial.

The famous portrait of the Chancellor can most interestingly be compared with the panel in the Kaiser Friedrich Museum at Berlin, which represents Etienne Chevalier, trésorier de France and favourite alike of Charles VII, Agnès Sorel and Louis XI, kneeling beside his patron Saint (Plate V). Here, again, we have an example of Foucquet's exceptional talent for the revelation of character, and at once we see in Etienne Chevalier the traits of a man of loyalty and intelligence, dignified in bearing, though oppressed and tired by the incessant strain of national affairs. Foucquet has represented the *trésorier* quietly kneeling beside St. Stephen, in an attitude of official devotion, with his hands clasped in prayer. The dignified but worldly figure of the Donor is strikingly contrasted with the ascetic, ethereal figure of the Saint, who places his right hand upon Etienne's shoulder and holds, in his left, the Gospel Book and the stone of his martyr-dom. The whole picture reveals a sharp, decided draughtsman-ship and everywhere the artist's technique is impeccable. The head of each of the figures is modelled in an intelligent and masterly fashion, and the stone which Saint Stephen carries on the book is portrayed with all the clear-cut brilliance of some facetted mineral, rare enough to be a collector's piece. The back-ground of the panel again reflects the influence of Italy and is con-ceived in the Renaissance style. Corinthian columns are again in evidence, and gold, once more, is discreetly and impressively used.

The design of the Kaiser Friedrich panel at once leads one to suspect that the picture is a fragment of some composite piece, and such a doubt is justified. The portrait of Etienne Chevalier, with his patron Saint, is the left-hand wing of the famous Melun Diptych, which hung in the church at Melun until 1775.

Most fortunately, the right-hand panel of this exquisite work has been identified and, thanks to an inscription, we know it to be the famous 'Virgin and Child' (Plate VI) (now at the Royal Gallery at Antwerp), which is said to be a portrait of Agnès Sorel, the King's acknowledged mistress and the protectress of Etienne Chevalier and one of the three executors of his will. There is, indeed, no definite proof that this identity is correct, but the portrait bears an undeniable likeness to the funeral effigy of Agnès at Loches. The model for Foucquet's Virgin has, moreover, a high forehead, a small mouth, a milk-white skin and perfectly rounded breasts, all of which were points of beauty of which Agnès was expressly proud. Agnès, if she it be, is a type of beauty essentially French: intelligent and aloof; she is clothed in a plain dress of greyish-blue and wears a mantle of the royal ermine. On her head, she has a magnificent crown of pearls and rubies. The throne on which she sits is also studded with precious stones, all of which are painted with extreme transparency and beauty. The delicacy of the technique is beyond reproach, and in the reflection of a window, seen in the ball of one of the tassels which adorn the throne, we have something with which Jan van Eyck himself might have been well pleased. The Virgin is supporting the Child upon her knee, and here, for once, the artist's technical achievement fails. The infant Jesus is as heavy as His Mother is exquisite, and were it not for the counter-balance of an assembly of red and blue angels who, like *putti*, cluster round the throne, the delicacy of the conception would be seriously impaired.

The first thought which strikes everyone who has seen both the Berlin and Antwerp panels is that the two pictures not only differ in style so greatly one from another, but fail as a design to make a complete whole. The difference in treatment is at once impressive; the figure of Etienne Chevalier in Berlin is realistically and robustly conceived, whereas the Antwerp Virgin is unreal and imaginative, and possesses a cool, unearthly pallor which makes us think not of Jehan Foucquet but of Piero della Francesca. There is, moreover, a slight difference in size: the Berlin panel is 4.7 cms. higher than its counterpart, which suggests that the Antwerp picture was subsequently reduced in size. The design, too, of the diptych seems incomplete and it has many times been suggested that the diptych, in its original form, was a triptych and that the third panel represented Catherine Budé, the wife of Etienne Chevalier, also perhaps with her patron Saint, kneeling in worship before the Virgin. But, tantalizing as this theory may sound, the suggestion is injudicious and there are no grounds for believing it to be true. The wife of Etienne Chevalier had died many years before this picture was painted (she died in 1452) and, what is more, she was never represented in any of the paintings in which her husband appeared, not even in the miniatures. Not even her coat-of-arms was ever included. It is not, therefore, likely that the lady's portrait would quite fortuitously have been included in the diptych of the church at Melun. If, indeed, there ever was a third panel—and its existence is highly improbable— it must have vanished during the seventeenth century, as in no records does its mention appear.[1]

Dr. Friedländer, in his article in the *Jahrbuch der Kgl. Preussischen Kunstsammlungen*, dates the painting of the diptych to the region of 1464. He also provides us with various significant quotations from certain early authorities and eye-witnesses of the master-piece in its original state. The most explicit authority is Denys Godefroi, who recorded his impressions towards the middle of

[1]Monsieur Henri Bouchot in an article in the *Revue de l'Art Ancien et Moderne* on the lost paintings of Jehan Foucquet persists in his opinion that a third panel existed and that it represented Catherine Budé in prayer. Only the discovery, however, of this legendary panel would prove the point.

Monsieur Bouchot in his article is both ingenious and provocative, since he has, by a careful study of mediaeval drawings and engravings of portrait subjects, amassed a collection of famous personages who may have sat to Foucquet or to members of his school. Among this galaxy of well-known names we find Alonso Tostas, Bishop of Avila; Jacques Cœur; Marie d'Anjou; Jean Michel, Bishop of Angers; Gilles de Rome; Jacques Binet, governor of Tours; and Jehan Dunois, the Bastard of Orleans.

the seventeenth century. He states that, on the occasion of his visit to the church at Melun, the diptych hung half-way up the wall behind the choir and near the sacristy. A later authority, on the other hand, tells us that the pictures hung above the door of the sacristy. This does not, however, imply that the position of the masterpiece was necessarily changed and is more likely to reveal an inaccuracy on the part of the earlier recorder, Godefroi.

But both accounts are unanimous in one respect: they both refer to the work as 'two pictures' and not as a double-panelled picture. It seems, therefore, that each section was separately framed and mounted, and that they hung, one beside the other. We have reason, moreover, to believe that each was protected by a curtain, for the reference states that 'chacun a un rideau qui le couvre'. The agreement on this point of the various references indicates that the work was not a diptych in the strict sense of the word, but two almost equi-sized and companion panels juxta-posed. It certainly was not a folding diptych like the famous example from Wilton House.

The references concerning these two panels are generous and they tell us something about the mounting. The pictures were evidently hung on a background of blue velvet which was decor-ated with gold and silver scrolls and *entrelacs* ornamented with two large E's (the initial of the donor) and studded with pearls. Around the frame of each section, there ran a decoration of small medallions of silver and gold, perhaps painted in enamel. Around the left-hand panel, were scenes from the life of St. Stephen and, on the right, scenes from the life of the Virgin.

The Melun Diptych—and particularly the section at Antwerp —may be considered as the highest point which our artist reached in those examples of portraiture which may, with reason, be attributed to him. The calm, sophisticated beauty of the Antwerp Virgin is unforgettable in its matchless delicacy and sensibility, and the entire work has an imaginative quality which brings it into line with the greatest pictures of all time.

But there is another portrait, almost certainly by our artist, in

PLATE XXIV (*see page* 71)
JESUS CARRYING THE CROSS
Hours of Etienne Chevalier
Chantilly: Musée Condé
[*to face page* 55]

which he achieves an extraordinary refinement of technique and subtlety of observation: The 'Portrait of a Man' in the Liechtenstein Gallery at Vienna (Plate VII). Here we see the representation of a young man of about 30 years of age, clean-shaven, with irregular features and curious eyes which reveal a slight squint. He is dressed in the simplest of costumes: a brown cap and a dress severe enough to be a monastic habit. At his neck he wears a clasp of exquisite jewelled metalwork. This portrait bears a close resemblance to the famous enamel medallion—said to be a self-portrait—in the Louvre. The type of the sitter is much the same, and there is, also, in both works, an inscription capriciously written in quaint and very similar characters. Dr. Friedländer was so much struck by the likeness between the two works that he regarded the Liechtenstein panel as another portrait of the artist. But Lafenestre, though admitting the similarity, inclines towards the perhaps more reasoned view that the sitter was not Jehan Foucquet himself but some relation; perhaps a cousin or brother.

The 'Portrait of a Man with a Wine Glass', formerly in the Wilzceck Collection at Vienna and now in the Louvre, was at one time thought to be by Foucquet, but, partly owing to the hard luminosity of the technique and intensity of execution, the suggestion has since been waived and the theory of Foucquet's authorship is now held only by very few.[1]

Apart from these famous panel pictures, there are a few portrait drawings which are with reason held by some to be by Foucquet. The most impressive of these is the well-known 'Roman Legate'—once in the Heseltine Collection and now in the possession of Mr. Henry Oppenheimer in London—and the Study for the Head of Jouvenel des Ursins in Berlin.[2] Another important

[1]In the possession of Messrs. Bottenweiser, Berlin, there is a portrait, said to be of the Comte Dunois, Bastard of Orleans, which bears a striking resemblance to Foucquet's work. In *Unknown Masterpieces* (Zwemmer, 1930) Mr. Valentiner has reproduced the portrait and has attributed it to Jehan Foucquet, drawing a comparison between it and the left-hand panel of the Melun Diptych in Berlin.

[2]See Appendix I and Plates L, LI.

drawing is the portrait of Mme. de Beaudricourt, formerly in the Collection of the Comte Durrieu.

It has several times been seen that Jehan Foucquet was celebrated for his painting on enamel but, unfortunately, very few examples of his talent in this direction remain to us and we have only two enamel medallions which can, with any justification, be attributed to Foucquet. It is possible, however, that his excursions into this sphere of art may have been by no means rare, since, for example, we know that the mounting of the Melun Diptych was adorned with an elaborate series of medallions painted on enamel.

The more famous—and by far the more important—of the two enamels attributed to Foucquet is the enamelled copper medallion, known as the Self-Portrait, in the Galerie d'Apollon at the Louvre (Plate VIII). This exquisite work has been much discussed from every point of view and the theory that it represents our artist himself has been greatly debated. Some there are who consider that the attribution of the medallion to Foucquet's authorship is dangerous and unlikely. Monsieur de Mely, a distinguished critic, forcibly opposed the theory of Foucquet's authorship and considered that the medallion was not French work of the fifteenth century but Italian of the sixteenth, basing his argument on the supposition that the particular kind of gilding which the medallion reveals was not invented until 1484 (three years after Foucquet's death) by a *faiencier*, Antonius Lollus, of the school of Abruzzi.

This objection is, however, open to question and, as Monsieur Marquet de Vasselot very readily suggested, even if this gilding was not applied in Foucquet's time to ceramic ware, it may well have been applied to copper, the medium of our medallion. The theory, moreover, of Lollus's invention is itself extremely uncertain and there is no direct evidence informing us either that he was the originator of the art of gilding on ceramics or that he lived in the sixteenth century. Some scholars, indeed, place his date as late as the seventeenth century.

The Louvre medallion bears the signature 'Johannes Fouquet',

PLATE XXV (*see page* 72)
THE DESCENT FROM THE CROSS
Hours of Etienne Chevalier
Chantilly: Musée Condé
[*to face page* 56]

which, again, has raised many doubts. Mely urged that this inscription did not authenticate the work to Foucquet but that it indicated, rather, the hand of an Italian of the sixteenth century, since a Frenchman of the preceding century would have been more likely to sign himself 'Jehan' than 'Johannes'. But, from the point of view of paleography, this inscription on the medallion tallies exactly with the inscriptions on the Hours of Etienne Chevalier at Chantilly and the fact of its latinization does not at all preclude it from the time of Foucquet. Latin inscriptions and latinized signatures (such as those of Jan Van Eyck and Jehan de Bruges) were common at that period, and the fact that Foucquet had been to Italy heightens the possibility of his having made this excursion into the classic tongue. Apart from the inscription, the little medallion has nothing which is reminiscent of Italy, and the type of the man's head is distinctly Tourangeau, with his short features and rather thick lips. Whether the portrait is of the artist himself or not is a difficult point to decide, but there seems no definite reason against this possibility, and, in fact, there are several points in its favour. We have only to compare the medallion with the well-known portrait in the Liechtenstein Gallery, and we see at once that the two types portrayed are very similar; it is, then, by no means unlikely—but, rather, very probable—that both the works are by Jehan Foucquet and represent portraits of himself and a kinsman.

The question inevitably arises as to where and from whom Jehan Foucquet learned the art of painting on enamel. It is, indeed, likely that he learnt it from his friend Filarète, whom we know of as the expert in enamelling who was commissioned to decorate with enamel medallions a bronze statue (now at Dresden) for Pietro di Medici.

Another medallion, attributed to our artist, is in the Kunstgewerbe Museum at Berlin, and represents the 'Believers and Disbelievers'. The medallion is circular in shape and depicts two groups of persons. On the left are the Jews, all of whom are bearded and wear turbans (a guise which Foucquet seems to have considered essentially Hebraic, as he often chose it for the Jews), and on the right are the Christians, clean-shaven, dressed in long robes, and devoutly receiving some celestial benefit.

The significance of this medallion is difficult to assess as it is obviously one of a series, and its character immediately promotes the suggestion that it formed part of the decoration which surrounded the Melun Diptych. Both the medallions, indeed, could, as regards size and general appearance, have formed part of this decoration but it seems unlikely that such subjects would have been chosen to ornament the mounting of the masterpiece at Melun. To decorate the panel of a picture of the Virgin with a portrait of oneself in enamel would have been a vanity with which Jehan Foucquet would have had little sympathy, and it does not seem any more likely that the 'Believers and Disbelievers' would have found a place in the artist's scheme. It is generally supposed that the medallion surrounding the Melun Diptych represented, on the one side, scenes from the Life of the Virgin and, on the other, a series from the Life of St. Stephen, and neither of these scenes would have included the subject of the Berlin medallion. The problem, therefore, of the origin of these two enamel masterpieces must remain unsolved, but they must still be regarded as of the greatest importance, not merely because of their intrinsic value but because of the likelihood that they are creations of Maistre Foucquet's master hand.

PLATE XXVI (*see page* 73)
DAVID IN PRAYER
Hours of Etienne Chevalier
Chantilly: Musée Condé
[to face page 58]

PART THREE

THE MINIATURES

CHAPTER SEVEN

RELIGIOUS BOOKS. AT CHANTILLY AND ELSEWHERE

I T I S with the decoration of religious books and Books of Hours
that the name of Jehan Foucquet is most generally associated,
and, in particular, with the painting of the famous *Hours of
Etienne Chevalier*, of which the greater part can be seen at Chantilly. It seems indeed strange that we have not more examples of
'Hours' from the hand of Foucquet, since it is highly probable that
he painted many books of this kind. Many examples, however,
have, unfortunately, not come down to us. The illumination of
Books of Hours was for the mediaeval painter the most lucrative
and secure means of livelihood, since all wealthy and aristocratic
people demanded a painted prayerbook, and even the more well-
to-do among the middle classes on occasion gave commissions.
It is, therefore, a just hypothesis to suppose that Foucquet and his
colleagues spent much time in executing this form of commission,
but, unluckily, examples in which we may safely say that Foucquet's hand has worked are rare.

There are various manuscripts, contemporary with our painter,
which contain one miniature suggesting the work of Foucquet and
others which are of a distinctly inferior quality. Such an example
is the Book of Hours, commissioned by Charles de France,
younger brother of Louis XI, now in the Bibliothèque Mazarine
in Paris (MS. No. 473). It contains a miniature ('The Kiss of
Judas') conceived very much in the master's style. Even nearer
than this to the Foucquet pattern are five or six miniatures in a
Book of Hours (*Le Livre d'Heures de la dernière Comtesse de
Flandres*) formerly in the Durrieu Collection. This book seems
to have been commissioned by Anne de Beaujeu-Amplepuis,

who married, as her second husband, Jehan de Beaudricourt, Maréchal de France. Two of the miniatures in this volume demand special attention: the 'Donor in prayer' and the 'Three Dead and the Three Living'.[1] The latter page, which strongly recalls the work of Foucquet, seems to have been famous in its day, since not only was it copied in paintings, but also it served as a model for an engraving inserted in a Dominican missal which was printed in Paris on the 28th February, 1518. At the Hague, moreover, there is a Book of Hours (A.A. 266) in which the miniature of the Crucifixion provokes an immediate comparison with Foucquet.[2]

But of all these sacred books, the one which most uniformly recalls Foucquet is to be found, somewhat surprisingly, at Sheffield in the John Ruskin Art Museum. It is the Book of Hours which, in the second half of the fifteenth century, was used by the Marquise Diane de Croy as an autograph album for her relatives and friends. Among the distinguished signatures which deface many of the pages can be found that of Mary Queen of Scots, second-cousin by marriage to the owner of the book. The exceptional similarity of this volume to the *Hours of Etienne Chevalier* at Chantilly was first observed by Dr. Sydney Cockerell, who most aptly pointed out its affinity with the more famous work, and, although not claiming that Foucquet was the artist, saw in it a kind of nutshell version of the Chantilly Hours. Similarities to that masterpiece and, in fact, to other works of Jehan Foucquet frequently occur within its pages, and one is constantly astonished by the discovery of deliberate reflections of miniatures both at Chantilly and elsewhere.

The book consists of 178 leaves and 20 full-page miniatures. The first, representing the Virgin and Child, attended by two praying angels, recalls the panel of Agnès Sorel at Antwerp; the

[1]Both these miniatures published in *La Peinture à l'Exposition des Primitifs Français*, by Comte Durrieu, Paris, 1904, frontispiece and p. 9.

[2]Reproduced in *Deux Miniatures inédites de Jean Foucquet*, Comte Durrieu, Paris, 1902. (Extract from *Mémoires de la Société des Antiquaires de France*.)

PLATE XXVII (*see page* 73)
A FUNERAL PROCESSION
Hours of Etienne Chevalier
Chantilly: Musée Condé
[*to face page* 63]

second is a beautiful imaginative conception of Saint John at Patmos; the third, 'The Mass of St. Gregory', is less satisfactory, the draughtsmanship being feeble and the colours being greatly faded, perhaps owing to the damaging habit of osculation; the fourth, 'The Annunciation' (Plate IX), recalls very forcibly the miniature of the 'Virgin and Child' (cp. Plates XVII, XVIII), in the Chantilly Hours, and is also reminiscent of the larger panel pictures in the Louvre and at Berlin. There is here a strong insistence upon gold as an architectural background, and again we see the artist's predilection for Corinthian columns and Italianate fluted pilasters. The fifth miniature represents the Visitation (Plate XII), and here the figures, standing in a tessellated courtyard (cp. the Holford and Etienne Chevalier Books of Hours. Plates XI, XX), wear curious turban-like headdresses which indicate most strongly an Italian influence. The Crucifixion, Pentecost and Trinity—the latter with its startling use of scarlet angels—all resemble strikingly the Chantilly Hours, whilst the ninth miniature, the Funeral Procession (Plate XIII), has a similarity to its counterpart in that famous work and also to a miniature in a Book of Hours at Copenhagen (cp. Plates XIV, XXVII) which is exceedingly impressive. Here in the facial expressions we recognize the blunt features of the *type tourangeau* such as we saw them in the Louvre enamel and the Vienna portrait. The Nativity, the Death and Coronation of the Virgin all directly resemble their counterparts at Chantilly, whereas the David and Goliath recalls the series of historical paintings in miniature, of which two exist in London (Collection of Mrs. Yates Thompson) and two are in the Louvre. The last miniature, representing Job and his wife, has a landscape background, which, in its subtlety of light effect, recalls the Chevalier masterpiece.

But with affinity of style and similar choice of subject the matter ends; the colours have a weakness and the technique reveals an amateurish touch and a vein of coarseness which could never be associated with the mature art of Jehan Foucquet, and the book, by its very likeness to the Chantilly Hours, could not be a work of his inexperienced youth. These Hours at Sheffield must be, indeed, the result of Focuquet's inspiration, but the work cannot be considered that of the master himself but the product of a member of his *atelier* at Tours.

Less uniformly similar to the Chantilly miniatures but much more likely to contain work by the master himself is the famous and richly illuminated Book of Hours formerly in the Holford Collection and now in the possession of Mr. Chester Beatty. At least two and perhaps three of the miniatures in this book are of such high excellence and reveal not only direct affinities to the Hours at Chantilly but such taste and consummate skill that the hand of Foucquet can hardly here be doubted. The Annunciation, for instance, with its chaste design and exquisite garden-vista, conforms entirely with Foucquet's highest standard. The miniature of the Visitation, moreover, with its delicious setting of the tessellated courtyard and its figures which both in costume and posture are almost exactly the counterparts of those in the Visitation at Chantilly, compels us to believe that Foucquet was its author (see Plates X, XI, XX).

Another Book of Hours which reminds us of Jehan Foucquet is that of the Cardinal Charles de Bourbon in the Royal Library at Copenhagen (G.K.S. 1610. 4°), a finely illuminated manuscript which was once in the possession of Philippe de Bethune, although not originally executed to meet with his commission. Dr. Winkler, in an article in the *Zeitschrift für bildende Kunst* (1919-20, pp. 195-206), has attributed the book to Foucquet, laying a special insistence upon various undeniable resemblances of style. He notes that a 'Pieta', compactly designed within an initial letter, reflects many of Foucquet's characteristic traits of form, line and characterization and it is evident that the miniature representing the Funeral Procession is directly related to its counterparts at Chantilly and Sheffield (see Plates XIII, XIV, XXVII). The likeness here, indeed, is so strong that the inspiration of Foucquet seems certain, but the fact that Foucquet's own hand was actually responsible for these miniatures seems less evident and very hard

PLATE XXVIII (see page 74)
JOB ON THE DUNGHEAP
Hours of Etienne Chevalier
Chantilly: Musée Condé
[*to face page 65*]

to prove. But the miniature from the same manuscript representing the Virgin and the Donor, which is also reproduced by Dr. Winkler in his article, seems less reminiscent of our artist and, for all its excellence of portraiture and purity of colour, it has a simplicity of design and setting which give a note of immaturity out of keeping with Foucquet's subtle mastery of the problems of pictorial technique.

By far the most famous and most precious Book of Hours by Jehan Foucquet is that known as the *Heures d'Etienne Chevalier*. Unhappily, the set of miniatures is not complete, since the volume was lacerated by some vandal's hand in the early years of the eighteenth century. The pages were torn from their binding, and at the base of some of the miniatures certain of the original detail was hidden either by a design of painted flowers or by an applied decoration, stuck on to the lower edge of Foucquet's page.

The greater part of the paintings have, fortunately, been kept together through a chain of circumstances which began with the purchase, in 1805, of forty miniatures by M. Georges Brentano-Laroche of Frankfurt-am-Main. They were sold to him by a merchant of Bâle for 5,000 francs. In 1891 M. Brentano's son, M. Louis Brentano, sold the miniatures for 250,000 francs to the Duc d'Aumale, who left them as part of the Musée Condé at Chantilly to become a national possession. Two other miniatures of the same series are in the Louvre; one is at the Bibliothèque Nationale; one is at the British Museum and another, discovered in 1923, is in a private collection in London.

The question of the authenticity of these marvellous works at once arises, and at once we find ourselves baffled for a definite answer. There is, indeed, no actual proof that Foucquet painted these, or any other miniatures for Etienne Chevalier, nor, in fact, is there a means of proving that Foucquet painted any of the works which are usually attributed to him except the *Antiquités Judaïques* which the librarian's note has definitely authenticated for us. But all scholars now agree that the connection of Jehan Foucquet with the Chevalier Hours is so likely as to be almost an established fact and that the doubts which certain *lacunae* of evidence must excite can justifiably be waived.[1]

Of one point we can be certain: the Hours were, without question, commissioned by Etienne Chevalier, since his name is mentioned on every page. The artist's politeness, indeed, seems, at times, exaggerated, since on each miniature the donor's name or initials or both appear. The portrait, moreover, of him who was to have the good fortune to possess the book is by no means rarely included in the series.

Etienne Chevalier was a statesman of considerable distinction and of unimpaired repute. The friend and counsellor of Charles VII and Louis XI, he was admitted to the inner circle of court confidence and never betrayed his trust. From 'secrétaire du roi' he became the King's financial adviser and finally, in 1452, he was elected to the supreme position of 'trésorier de la France'. He was, therefore, a man of no mean dignity and a personage whose prayer-book was not unfittingly embellished by the work of a master-painter.

It has been seen that the miniatures were taken from their setting and haphazardly disposed of. The question, then, arises of their order. M. Gruyer in *Les quarante Foucquet* considers that the order of the miniatures should follow the chronological sequence of events, but M. Henri Martin, in his admirable brochure on the subject of the Chantilly Hours, is of the opinion that a chronological order would be fitting for a succession of small paintings, but not for a series of miniatures adorning the Hours of Prayer.

[1]For many years no name was attributed to the miniatures. In 1833 Passavant mentioned them but left them anonymous. In 1835 G. K. Nagler published the volume of his great lexicon of artists containing letter F, and omitted Foucquet. In 1836 the Comte Raczinski tried to unravel an inscription which appears in the miniature representing the Stoning of St. Stephen and came to the audacious conclusion that the artist's name was Viwoar Hskatus, remarking on the strangeness that an artist of such great brilliance and one bearing this unusual name should have been forgotten! It was Waagen, however, who first launched the attribution to Foucquet and saw in the Hours a likeness to the *Antiquités Judaïques*.

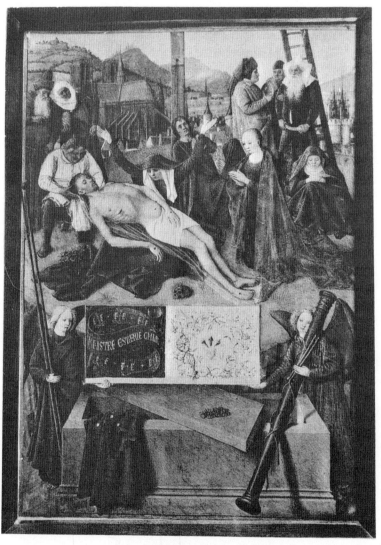

PLATE XXIX (*see page* 74)
STABAT MATER DOLOROSA
Hours of Etienne Chevalier
Chantilly: Musée Condé
[*to face page* 66]

He has, therefore, classified the miniatures according to the divisions of the Liturgy.

A Book of Hours must inevitably begin with a *Calendar*, in which each month is usually decorated with two miniatures, the one depicting the sign of the Zodiac and the other the occupation characteristic of the month. Unfortunately, the calendar of the *Hours of Etienne Chevalier* has never been traced and is one of our most serious losses.

Next come the passages from the *Four Evangelists*; these never change but are submitted to an inflexible rule and are always chosen from Saint John i. 1-14; Saint Luke i. 26-38; Saint Matthew ii. 1-12; Saint Mark xvi. 14-20. The customary decoration with which to adorn each of these passages is a figure of the Evangelist, writing, accompanied by his attribute. But Foucquet thought fit, except in the case of St. John whom he represents writing accompanied by his eagle on the island of Patmos (Plate XV), to depart from the rigidity of tradition. For St. Matthew he substituted the Adoration of the Magi (Plate XVI) (a famous miniature in which the figure of the King, kneeling before the Virgin on a cloth of *Fleur de Lys*, is none other than Charles VII himself[1]) and for St. Mark he chose the Ascension. Of his treatment of the passages from St. Luke we cannot speak, since the page has disappeared.

Following on the passages from the Evangelists are the two *Devotions of the Virgin*, the one beginning *Obsecro te Domina* and the other *O intemerata*. The first is usually decorated with a representation of the Virgin and Child and the second by a Mater Dolorosa. In the *Hours of Etienne Chevalier* we have the first (Plates XVII, XVIII) but of the second there is no trace. In Foucquet's miniature the Virgin is sitting, nursing the Child, before the

---

[1]The battle scene which is in progress in the background of this miniature makes a grotesque contrast with the peaceful incidents of the foreground. But no real engagement is represented—merely the sham manœuvres and make-believe attacks upon the city which formed part of the programme of traditional feasts in honour of Epiphany.

porch of a cathedral, which, strangely, seems to be situated at the end of a large hall. Here we have a mixture of styles, French and Italian, since the cathedral porch is Gothic, whereas the walls of the hall are undoubtedly Italian, with their panels of coloured marble, their Corinthian columns, and a frieze of *putti* bearing garlands. Before Our Lady kneel the angel host and at their head kneels St. Stephen, stone in hand, presenting the donor, Etienne Chevalier, to the Virgin. This miniature, undeniably the finest in the series, may have been placed at the head of the volume, immediately after the Calendar.

After these three preliminary sections, the Hours, proper, begin. The Hours are of three kinds, and are divided into the following classes: The Hours of the Virgin or of Our Lady, The Hours of the Cross or of the Passion, and the Hours of the Holy Ghost. The Hours of the Virgin usually comprise eight parts, each of which should be decorated with a miniature, whilst the Hours of the Cross and those of the Holy Ghost generally are a little shorter and consist of seven parts.

Foucquet's selection of subject matter in the *Hours of the Virgin* is not completely orthodox and in certain of the divisions he has departed from the general rule. For *Matins, Lauds and Prime*, however, he has conformed to the traditional representations of the Annunciation, Visitation and Nativity. In each case the setting is interesting and in many of the miniatures there is a certain topographical element which provokes comment. In the miniature of the Annunciation (Plate XIX), for instance, the Virgin receives the Tidings in a church which can, perhaps, be identified with the Sainte Chapelle at Paris or the Sainte Chapelle at Bourges, a setting which gives the miniature an atmosphere which is Gothic and completely French. At the base are the opening words of Matins: *Domine, labia mea aperies. . . .* Its successor, however, the miniature of the Visitation (Plate XX), reveals a completely different style and here we catch a glimpse of Foucquet's colourful imagination and beautiful variety. Mary and Elizabeth are meeting, not in France, but in Italy; they stand in the courtyard of a rich Italian house before a portico supported by four Corinthian columns. In the left background a man is drawing water from a well, whilst a little child is splashing his hands on the water's surface. The courtyard door is open and leads into an avenue of cypress trees. Elizabeth is attended by Zachariah and a handmaid who is wearing an elaborate turbaned costume (cp. the Sheffield and the Holford Books of Hours; Plates XI, XII) which can only be Italian in design. The pediment of the portico bears the donor's name and initials (Maistre Etienne Chevalier, E.C.) and at the base of the miniature are the opening words of Lauds: *Deus in adjutorium meum intende.* . . . The third miniature, the Nativity (Plate XXI), brings us back again to France and at once we see that the shepherds, who marvel at the event which has honoured the humble stall and even the dog which patiently awaits their ecstasy to pass, have come directly from the pasture-lands of the Loire. The base of the miniature is again inscribed with the opening words of Prime: *Deus in adjutorium meum intende.* . . .

For *Terce*, Foucquet has somewhat strangely departed from the general rule, and instead of portraying the Tidings to the shepherds (an incident which he included in the background of the preceding miniature), he chose to paint a second 'Annunciation'. This time, the Virgin receives the Messenger not in church but in her room, of which the furnishing is curiously hybrid. The ceiling of oak beams is French but the walls, with their coloured marble panels, supported by Corinthian columns, are entirely Italian in fashion. The Virgin's bed, moreover, is Flemish in design with its overhanging canopy and looped-up curtain, and it at once evokes comparison with Van Eyck and Rogier van der Weyden. As in nearly every case, the base of the miniature is adorned with the opening words of the liturgical section to which it is the complement.

For *Sext*, Foucquet has again deserted the conventions, and instead of choosing one of the more usual subjects (either the Adoration of the Magi or their visit to Herod), he selected 'The Death of the Virgin'. The Virgin, attended on her death-bed by

St. John and St. Peter who sprinkle Her with holy water, is being received among the saints by Jesus who, in a mandorla of angels, receives Her soul.

For *Nones*, Foucquet chose 'The Funeral of the Virgin' rather than conform to the traditional subject.[1] The Virgin's bier is being carried by the Apostles through a landscape which has much resemblance to the region of the Loire.

For *Vespers*, we have the 'Assumption of the Virgin',[2] which in general style and aspect resembles the miniature for the *Sext*.

The final division of the 'Hours of the Virgin', that of *Compline*, brings us back once more to the fold of orthodoxy, since Foucquet has here traditionally represented the Virgin's Coronation (Plate XXII). In this marvellous miniature we see the tripartal Throne of the Three Persons of the Trinity. Foucquet has represented the Three Persons as all alike and of the same age. God the Father and God the Holy Ghost sit on the Throne, but God the Son, having put down the orb which He was holding, has left His place to crown His Mother as Queen of Heaven. On either side of the Throne is a three-tiered company of scarlet angels.

This miniature contains many stylistic elements which remind us of Foucquet's Italian journey: the throne is adorned with a frieze of garlanded *putti* and the pavement on which the Virgin kneels is of handsome Italian tile-work.

After the 'Hours of the Virgin' come the *Hours of the Cross*, which comprise seven liturgical divisions. In this section, Foucquet has not at all transgressed the border-line of custom and in each case his subject conforms to the traditional rule.

For *Matins*, the conventional illustration is the 'Arrest of Jesus at Gethsemane' (Plate XXIII), and here Foucquet has given us his first representation of a night scene. The artist's conception of the event is human and dramatic; two of the soldiers who crowd in at the gate carry flaming torches whilst an old woman holds up a

[1]Either the Purification, Circumcision, or, rarely, the Flight into Egypt.

[2]Again unconventional. The rule demands the Flight into Egypt or the Massacre of the Innocents.

PLATE XXX (*see page* 75)
THE TRINITY IN GLORY
Hours of Etienne Chevalier
Chantilly: Musée Condé
[*to face page* 71]

lantern lest there should be any mistake in the identity of the Prisoner. On the left, the terror-stricken young man, mentioned by Saint Mark, is running away. This miniature has the additional decoration of an illuminated letter D (the initial letter of Matins: *Domine labia mea aperies . . .*). In the central space of the letter, is a representation of Jesus praying on the Mount of Olives whilst the Apostles sleep.

The miniature for *Prime* depicts 'Jesus before Pilate'. In the upper half of the picture Jesus stands before the Procurator in a magnificent hall, of which the walls again display Foucquet's favourite device of marble panels and Corinthian columns. It is evident that Pilate and not Caiaphas is represented, since the inscription on the frieze which surrounds the room reads: 'Senatus populusque Romanus', and the shields with which the walls are hung bear its abbreviated counterpart, 'S.P.Q.R.' Pilate, himself, is seated on a throne, whilst Caiaphas, in robes and mitre, stands in the centre of the scene. Below, two carpenters, copied by Foucquet in all likelihood from actual citizens of Tours, are busy-making the Cross. On the right, a guard is releasing Barabbas from prison. The illuminated letter D (which opens the division of Prime) contains a portrayal of the Flagellation.

The division of *Terce* of the 'Hours of the Cross', which would probably have been represented by the 'Ecce Homo', is lost, but the miniature for *Sext* represents 'Jesus carrying the Cross' (Plate XXIV). The procession passes before a moated city, in the midst of which can be seen the Palais and the Sainte Chapelle of Paris. In the background, a devil flies away with the soul of Judas who is hanging, disembowelled, from a tree. In the immediate foreground, a guard is picking up two nails from the ground whilst an old woman—in a white apron and having the appearance of a homely Tourangelle—is ferociously forging the third. The illuminated letter D contains a picture of Saint Veronica with the imprinted handkerchief.

Nones have as their illustration the 'Crucifixion', and in his conception of this scene, Foucquet has adhered to the orthodox.

71

The ferocity of the crowd is admirably portrayed and a touch of realism is seen in the representation of the soldier offering Jesus, high upon the Cross, the sponge of gall. In the foreground, the soldiers are engaged in their lottery for Jesus's clothes.

The division of *Vespers* is represented by the 'Descent from the Cross' (Plate XXV), and here the setting is completely Italian. The tragic incident is taking place before an Italian town, in which can be plainly seen a round domed building, resembling a baptistery. As yet, this building, which occurs again in the succeeding miniature, has never been identified. Some scholars have claimed it as a building in Ravenna; others have assigned it to an edifice in Bergamo, but certainty has never resulted from their argument.

The division of *Compline*, which concludes these solemn Hours, has a miniature representing the 'Embalmment of the Body of Jesus', which is less commonly portrayed than the familiar Entombment. Here the setting is strangely hybrid; in the background we see again the Italian city with the domed building, but on the left is a turreted house of Tours, along which a charming pergola of fruit trees is trained. At Jesus's feet, in the presence of disciples and saints, kneels Etienne Chevalier.

The final section of the Hours proper, the *Hours of the Holy Ghost*, is divided usually into seven parts, but it is very rare that all these sections should be illustrated. Usually—perhaps because the artists found this section too vague for actual representation—there is only one miniature, at the head of Matins, depicting Pentecost.

But Foucquet has been very generous in his decoration of this portion of the book and has adorned it with three miniatures. For *Prime* (as is more usual when more than one division is illustrated) he has chosen Pentecost. The setting here is definitely Italian and the Virgin, with the Apostles, receives the Holy Spirit in a magnificent marble hall.

The division of *Nones* has as its ornament the 'Spring of the Apostles'. Here again, the dominant note is one of Italy. The

PLATE XXXI (*see page* 77)
THE MARTYRDOM OF SAINT APOLLINA
Hours of Etienne Chevalier
Chantilly: Musée Condé
[*to face page* 72]

fountain, most elaborately carved, stands in a marble court of which the wall is inlaid with coloured panels and decorated with fluted Corinthian pilasters. Above, *putti* bear the escutcheons of the donor, whose initials are also imprinted on alternate tiles on the ground of the courtyard. A mark of Foucquet's elastic imagination is shown in the representation of a globe of fire, suspended in mid air, which sheds its rays upon the assembled Apostles.

Compline of the 'Hours of the Holy Ghost' has, as its pictorial complement, the 'Ascension of the Holy Ghost' which in the form of a dove returns to Jesus in glory, bearing the *lucerna mundi*.

The Hours, proper, are now completed and out of the approximate twenty-two miniatures which once completed the series, seventeen remain.

The next division of the Liturgy is the *Office of the Virgin*— the Office which immediately precedes Advent. The picture which accompanies this Office usually represents some important event in the life of the Virgin and Foucquet has chosen the scene of Her marriage. The ceremony—of which the culmination was the flowering of Joseph's staff—is taking place before a Roman triumphal arch, representing, as the Latin inscription tells us, the Temple of Solomon. Above the arch is inscribed the name of Etienne Chevalier.

The Virgin's office is followed by the *Seven Penitential Psalms* and the Litanies. The picture usually chosen for this division is an incident in the life of King David. Foucquet has represented David on the field of battle praying before a vision of God in Majesty (Plate XXVI). This miniature is not among the set at Chantilly but in the Department of Manuscripts in the British Museum.

With the next miniature, which illustrates the *Vespers of the Dead*, we see a Funeral Procession (Plate XXVII).[1] The cortege is passing through the square of a turreted town and at once our eye is attracted to the variety of the architecture. Most of the buildings are French Gothic, but there are two towers which

[1]Cp. Plates XIII, XIV, to which this miniature is closely allied.

immediately recall Foucquet's Italian journey. Above the left-hand side of the Square, rises a building very like the tower of the Palazzo Vecchio in Florence, and next to it is one which is strangely similar to the towers at Bologna or San Gimignano.

The funeral procession consists of priests and penitents. On the tapers which they carry and on the pall which covers the bier are the initials of Etienne Chevalier.

For his illustration of the *Vigil of the Dead*[1] Foucquet depicts, according to convention, Job on the Dungheap (Plate XXVIII). The most interesting element in this picture is the landscape background which gives us an unusual view of the Donjon de Vincennes.

The section following the Vigil should be the *Fifteen Joys of Mary*, but Foucquet's illustration for this portion has been lost and we pass immediately on to the *Stabat Mater Dolorosa* (Plate XXIX). The conventional representation of this scene is that of the Virgin standing before the Cross on which Christ is hanging, but Foucquet has here allowed his dramatic sense to have full sway and has portrayed the Virgin with the dead Christ on Her knees, lamenting over His body in an attitude of passionate, soul-destroying grief. This figure of the Virgin, with Her arms flung apart in wild despair, invites comparison with the figure of the Magdalene in Masaccio's Crucifixion. In the background is a view of Notre Dame de Paris and the Montagne Sainte Geneviève.

The *Seven Requests* are here represented by the nine verses of St. Bernard. Foucquet has portrayed the Saint in a cloister, surrounded by members of his order. Below, the Saint resists the onslaughts of the Devil.

This miniature of Saint Bernard now brings us on to the final portion of the book: the *Memoriae of the Saints*. Each saint is usually represented by an Antiphon and Prayer, and the section is very often preceded by an 'Antiphon and Prayer of the Trinity'. A great variety of saints is usually chosen with a view to the

[1]This section usually precedes the Vespers, but the reversal practised by Foucquet is not unique.

PLATE XXXII (see page 82)
STATUTES OF THE ORDER OF ST. MICHAEL
Paris: Bibliothèque Nationale (MS. fr. 19819)
[to face page 74]

region in which the Book of Hours was painted and the tastes of the patron by whom it was commissioned. Certain saints, however, must be included such as SS. Michael, John the Baptist, John the Evangelist, Peter and Paul; SS. Catherine, Barbara, Anna and the Magdalene.

Foucquet heralds the opening of the Memoriae by an *Antiphon* and *Prayer of the Holy Trinity* (Plate XXX). The three Persons of the Trinity (again all alike[1]), seated on their Throne with the Virgin separately enthroned nearby, are seen through what can only be described as a tunnel of radiant angels.

St. John the Baptist is represented by a miniature of the 'Birth of the Saint'. Here we see Foucquet in a more domestic mood and the first ablutions of the new-born child, watched by a group of admiring ladies who crowd into the room and stand around the mother's bed, might be an event in the life of some respected citizeness of Tours.

St. Peter is represented by a miniature of his Martyrdom, an impressive exercise in grim realism, and St. Paul by his Conversion. The painting devoted to St. Andrew reveals again a scene of martyrdom, and the soul of the Saint is seen leaving his tortured body in the form of a little child. In the foreground is a river with some people in a boat, who appear to bear no relation to the happenings on the bank. The pictorial tribute paid to St. James the Great, which follows the Crucifixion of St. Andrew, is yet another miniature of martyrdom, in which the Saint is being decapitated in the presence of Herod Agrippa.

With the representation of Saint John we are confronted with a less violent although hardly less dramatic scene, and here we see the Saint at the Last Supper, reposing on the breast of the Saviour, who is offering the bread to Judas. Through the door of the Upper Chamber is a church which recalls the style of Notre Dame de Paris.

The two succeeding miniatures, the Stoning of St. Stephen and the Ordination of St. Nicholas, have no special characteristics

[1] Cp. Compline of *Hours of the Virgin*, Pl. XXII.

75

upon which to comment, but the illustration representing St. Hilary in Council has a diverting decoration, added in a vignette, of the Saint on the island of Callinaria, driving away serpents and monsters.

The miniature representing St. Martin shows us the Saint performing an act of charity by cutting his coat in half to give a beggar. The scene is set on a bridge outside the gates of Amiens and the artist allows us a delicious view of the city, with its timbered houses overhanging the river's edge. This miniature is not at Chantilly but in the Louvre.

The remaining miniatures of the Chantilly series concern the female saints. The Antiphon of the Magdalene is illustrated by the washing by the Saint of Our Lord's Feet; the figures are seated in a vaulted refectory such as Foucquet must many times have seen during his Italian wanderings.

The 'Martyrdom of St. Catherine of Alexandria' which complements the Antiphon of that Saint, has an interesting setting and landscape background. On the left is a gibbet, possibly that of Montfaucon, and on the right is a castellated palace, perhaps the 'Temple' at Paris.

Next in order to this miniature, according to the classification of M. Henri Martin, come two paintings, both representing scenes from the life of female saints, which are not to be seen at Chantilly.

The former, which represents 'Saint Margaret and Olibrius', is in the Louvre; the latter is in the Bibliothèque Nationale. It was customary for artists, when depicting a scene from the life of Saint Margaret, to portray her in the process of being disgorged from the monster's jaws, but Foucquet preferred to choose a quieter theme and has represented the Saint, distaff in hand, guarding her flock outside the city walls and talking to her companions, whilst the Prefect Olibrius and his suite are arriving to arrest her. This miniature has, unluckily, been cut, and the opening words of the Antiphon of Saint Margaret (*Erat autem Margarita*) which undoubtedly existed have been torn away. The mutilation of the page caused a certain misunderstanding to arise concerning the subject of the miniature, and it was at one time thought to represent Saint Geneviève. Comte Durrieu, however, launched the theory that the subject was the surprise of Saint Margaret, and suggested that in the capital E which had been torn away, or in some portion of the lower half of the picture, Foucquet had painted a minute representation of the Saint's martyrdom and miraculous escape. The companion piece to the miniature of Saint Margaret is the 'Saint Anne and the Three Maries' in the Bibliothèque Nationale. The Saint and her three daughters stand, with their children, in a delicious pergola beyond which we can see the houses of a city and its cathedral. Far back, hidden in the depths of the pergola, is Joseph. Various attempts have been made to identify the cathedral; it seems most likely to be one of the smaller cathedrals in the region of the Loire, but hitherto its identity has not been traced.

The final miniature which concludes the *Hours of Etienne Chevalier* such as they are represented in the French Collections, is the 'Martyrdom of Saint Apollina' (Plate XXXI). This contains an extremely interesting representation of a contemporary *mystère* or religious play. The spectators are seen sitting round the stage in a row of tiered boxes. On the left is a staircase representing Heaven, on which sit two angels; in the foreground is a jester, who makes a grotesque contrast with the grim spectacle of saintly martyrdom which is being enacted in the centre of the stage. Four executioners are torturing the Saint whilst the King, who has left his box in the centre of the tier, goads them on to complete their work. The stage director, with a book in one hand and a baton in the other, conducts the music and gives orders to the actors.

Many suggestions have been made as to the reason of the artist's sudden whim to present his subject in the form of a mystery play, but the caprice is not so quixotic as at first it might appear since it was about this time, in 1461, that Foucquet was preparing a *mystère* for Louis XI. The scheme of theatrical performances would, therefore, have been continually revolving in his mind and his activities as impresario might well find reflection in his art, which was always as personal as it was exquisite.

The *Livre d'Heures d'Etienne Chevalier* is by no means complete and M. Martin assesses the missing leaves at thirteen or more.[1] Of recent years, the number of *lacunæ* has been reduced by one through the discovery in 1923 of the miniature representing St. Michael. This plate, which undoubtedly belongs to the series at Chantilly and bears the initials of Etienne Chevalier, was sold in London by Messrs. Maggs in the year of its discovery and is now in the possession of a private owner.[2]

In one point does this single page differ from the miniatures in the Musée Condé and in the Louvre: there the leaves are stuck to pieces of wood so that the reverse side is invisible, but in the case of the newly-found leaf, no such vandalism has been enacted and the reverse side, which reveals the text of a prayer referring to the illness of King Hezekiah (Isaiah xxxviii), can be read. The only way in which the miniature has been impaired is by the addition of a piece of ornamented margin from another manuscript, defacing the lines of text.

The miniature represents the familiar scene of St. Michael slaying the monster. St. Michael is wearing a breastplate in the shape of a cockle shell, which refers directly to the 'coquille de Saint Jacques': the emblem of Mont Saint Michel and an essential factor of the heraldic device of the famous Abbey of whose order Louis XI was the founder. In the inclusion of the cockle shell into St.

---

[1]The missing leaves are as follows: (*a*) The Calendar, (*b*) Gospel of St. Luke, (*c*) Mater Dolorosa (2nd Devotion of the Virgin), (*d*) Terce of Hours of the Cross, (*e*) Matins of Hours of the Holy Ghost, (*f*) Terce of Hours of the Holy Ghost, (*g*) Sext of Hours of the Holy Ghost, (*h*) Vespers of Hours of the Holy Ghost, (*i*) Lauds of Hours of the Cross, (*j*) Lauds of Hours of the Holy Ghost, and an indefinite number of the 'Memoriae of the Saints': perhaps as many as six.

[2]Reproduced in *Les Fouquet de Chantilly*, by Henry Martin, Paris, 1926, and *Livre d'Heures de J. F. . . . Le 45ième feuillet, retrouvé à Londres . . .*, by Comte Durrieu, 1923.

PLATE XXXIII (*see page* 83)
THE CORONATION OF CHARLEMAGNE
Grandes Chroniques de France
Paris: Bibliothèque Nationale (MS. fr. 6465)
[*to face page* 79]

Michael's breastplate, Foucquet is giving us a subtle reflection of the work which he undertook for Louis in the creation of the Order. The cockle shell appears again in the Statutes of the Order of St. Michael, of which Foucquet painted the frontispiece.

Comte Durrieu, in his pamphlet which concerns the discovery of this remarkable miniature and which includes a reproduction of the work, was the first to notice its iconographical affinity with Mont Saint Michel and he continued his discussion with other illuminating observations on points of detail. He remarks that the little round shield (bearing the combined initials of the Saint and the donor) was a common attribute in the fifteenth century of Saint Michael and he recalls an echo of it in the Van Eyck altarpiece at Ghent.

The monster with which the Saint is engaged is seven-headed —a fact which indicates that Foucquet had followed the Biblical text (Rev. xii. 3, 7-9), not keeping to the conventional version of the incident where the beast has only one head. Peeping over the rocks behind the monster is the head of another dragon: perhaps the anxious mate! Below, is a vision of Hell in which the dragon reappears, surrounded by flames, and two demons are torturing the souls of the damned. On the extreme left sits Lucifer, with little demons flying all around him.

In this miniature, Foucquet has departed somewhat from his usual naturalistic style and has explored the regions of fantasy. The result is not entirely happy, for Foucquet's strongest point was not the flight of imagination but a marvellous appreciation of the values of nature and of the things around him. As draughtsman and colourist, and for his management of complicated grouping, he is unsurpassed; and in all which entails an engaging realism, Foucquet is supreme. But with matters unterrestrial Foucquet felt ill at ease and his Saint Michael is no celestial being, but an ordinary soldier with wings attached; his seven-headed dragon, moreover, is not particularly fearsome and might as well be a gaggle of geese. It is not, indeed, in poetic or fanciful visions that Jehan Foucquet excels, but in the observation of character and the human mood; in the swift appreciation of dramatic elements; and in the representation of delicious landscapes, which have colours so pure that beside them the bluest sky seems dull and even the sunlight is dim.

PLATE XXXIV (*see page* 83)
BATTLE BETWEEN ROMANS AND CARTHAGINIANS
(CANNAE)
Paris: Musée du Louvre
[*to face page* 81]

CHAPTER EIGHT

SECULAR BOOKS. AT MUNICH AND ELSEWHERE

F OUCQUET'S ACTIVITIES in the decoration of precious books were not confined to religious subjects and there are various works of secular interest which can reasonably be attributed to the master of the Chantilly Hours and to the 'bon peintre' of the *Antiquités Judaïques*.

It has been seen that Foucquet, during his time of office as illuminator to the King, assisted Louis XI in the organization of the 'Ordre des Chevaliers de Saint Michel'. The Statutes of the Order, elaborately inscribed and presented in the form of a precious book, were decorated with a frontispiece by Foucquet and there is also evidence (given by Briçonnet) that our artist painted panel pictures—most likely portraits—for the Order. Of the larger works, unhappily, there is no trace, but the *Statuts de l'Ordre de Saint Michel* were discovered by the Comte Durrieu in the Bibliothèque Nationale (MS. fr. 19819).

For information concerning this manuscript, we have to thank Jehan Robertet, the father of the epoch-making annotator of the *Antiquités Judaïques* and the steward (*greffier*) of the Order of Saint Michael. Robertet states that Louis XI ordered a copy of the Statutes to be drawn up in book form, with a painted frontispiece representing himself as Founder of the Order surrounded by the principal Knights.

This connection of Foucquet with the steward of the Order of Saint Michael establishes for the first time the relation between the artist and the family of Robertet. That they should have been on friendly terms is by no means surprising, since Jehan Robertet was a fine scholar and a lover of the arts; he studied closely the recent developments in painting and expressed admiration for the work of Perugino and Rogier van der Weyden.

There is very little doubt that the miniature which heralds the text of St. Michael's statutes is by Foucquet (Plate XXXII). The likenesses of style, technique and colouring to the other works which we consider by our artist are astonishing and impressive. The picture is conceived entirely according to Louis' commission. The King is in the centre, attended by the Knights of his Order: Duc Charles de Guyenne (brother of Louis XI); Duc Louis II of Bourbon; the Comte de Roussillon, amiral de France; le Grand Maître Antoine de Chabannes, Jehan Bourré and others. In the back of the picture, the artist has courteously included a portrait of the steward, Jehan Robertet.

Another manuscript, also in the Bibliothèque Nationale, which can most logically be attributed to Jehan Foucquet is the *Grandes Chroniques de France* (MS. fr. 6465), which contains fifty miniatures of small size (fitting into one of the two columns of text) and one of larger dimensions. All the miniatures in this book are of the highest quality and present such a striking artistic excellence that, even as early as 1838, le Comte de Bastard suggested that they were from Foucquet's hand. There is not, indeed, much doubt that Foucquet played a large part in the decoration of this manuscript, although glimpses of a feebler hand can at times be seen. The dominant characteristics of our artist are there at once apparent: the marvellous talent for the values of composition; the excellent manipulation of the groups; the refined and poignant characterization; the dignity of bearing and natural gesture; a feeling for precious stuffs and a love of *hachures d'or*; views of cities and rivers; stretches of green pasture land and measureless expanses of azure sky. All these, indeed, are there in great abundance.

The paintings reveal, moreover, a significant topographical element which we associate with Foucquet. During the course of its pages we catch a glimpse of various churches, castles, towns and cities: Clichy, Montpensier, Orleans, Paris, Rheims, Tours

a feconde ptie de ce pnt liure terminee et ex
pedtee en laquelle eft touche le ʒouuerne
ment du ʒouuerncel en leftat moyen nom
me leconomique. Aeffe la derremere et tierce
purtie en laquelle feru truictie le ʒouuerne
ment dudit ʒouuerncel ou pluffimlt eftat nôme politique

PLATE XXXV (*see page* 84)
THE INVESTITURE OF JOUVENCEL BY LOUIS XI
Attributed to Foucquet
Wolfenbüttel: Herzog August Bibliothek (Cod. 137)
[*to face page* 82]

and others all appear therein. Our artist's vision is not, moreover, confined to France, and Tunis and Constantinople—both resembling French castellated cities—are given their due place. But the most interesting of the miniatures from the topographical view-point is 'The Crowning of Charlemagne on Christmas Day, 800, by Pope Leo III in St. Peter's at Rome' (Plate XXXIII). Here we have an exact representation of the Cathedral, not as we know it now but as Foucquet knew it during his sojourn in Rome. This miniature, then, provides us with an archeological document of the highest importance, and is one of our most accurate means of judging the appearance of the Church of St. Peter when it was still the ancient Basilica of Constantine.

A similar historical manuscript, of less importance than the *Chroniques* but, nevertheless, of considerable interest, is the *Histoire Ancienne jusqu'à Jules César et des Faits des Romains*. Of this document four full-sized miniatures survive. Two of them (representing 'Julius Caesar about to cross the Rubicon' and 'Pompey escaping after his defeat at Pharsalia') are in the possession of Mrs. Yates Thompson in London and two (representing the 'Coronation of Alexander' and a 'Battle between the Romans and Carthaginians') (Plate XXXIV) are in the Louvre. These four miniatures reveal very strongly certain characteristics both of colour and technique which we associate with Foucquet: the grouping of the figures is still supremely mastered; the penchant towards *hachures d'or* in the portrayal of the armour is persistently noticeable and the landscape backgrounds still reveal delicious glimpses of green fields and winding waters. If these pages are not by Foucquet himself—and they are hardly below the master's highest standard—they are certainly among the finest products of the school which we know Jehan Foucquet must have had. In the Middle Ages, all master painters became the nucleus of a group of pupils and assistants (*varlets: famuli*) and it is likely that Foucquet both employed many helpers and attracted a large number of apprentices.

There are some illuminated books in which the hand of Foucquet almost certainly played a part but which, in quality, are uneven; it is, then, safe to take the definite conclusion that in the inferior passages the pupils' work and not the master's is revealed.

An important work, which can be attributed to Foucquet, is the *Estrif de Vertu et Fortune* in the State Library at Leningrad. Monsieur Durrieu was the first to observe that the frontispiece, representing the allegorical figures of Virtue and Fortune, had much affinity with the *Antiquités Judaïques* and could with reason be considered as part of Foucquet's *œuvre*.

Another book which has recently been attributed to our artist is the copy of the *Jouvencel* (Cod. 137) at the Herzog August Bibliothek at Wolfenbüttel. The *Jouvencel* was a highly successful treatise by the courtier Jehan de Breuil, written expressly 'pour introduire et donner courage et hardement à tous les jeunes hommes qui ont le désir et voulenté de suivre le noble stille et exercices des armes'. Dr. Winkler in his article in the *Zeitschrift für Bildende Kunst* (1927-8, pp. 345-9) gives the work to Foucquet, but it is difficult to suppose that his attribution is correct. The page representing the 'Investiture of the Knight by Louis XI' (Plate XXXV) has many points of style which link it up with Foucquet and is certainly of the Foucquet School, but the consummate sureness of the master's hand seems absent. The figure of the kneeling knight has considerable grace both of conception and design, but the other figures, particularly the women who stand behind the King, are portrayed with a touch of coarseness and with an amateurish inefficiency which it is hard to associate with our artist. The view through the window, moreover, is feebly depicted although it presents just such an opportunity for engaging draughtsmanship by which Foucquet would have gladly profited.

The most celebrated of all the secular books of which the decoration has been attributed to Foucquet is the *Boccace de Munich*.[1] The title by which this book is always known is at once misleading, for the text does not represent the original writings of

[1] Cod. Gall. 369 Munich Staatsbibliothek.

Giovanni Boccaccio but is an arrangement into the French language by a certain Laurent de Premierfait of a treatise composed by Boccaccio in Latin: *De Casibus Virorum et Mulierum Illustrium* (*Des Cas des Nobles Hommes et Femmes Malheureux*).

The Munich manuscript is of French origin; it was copied on 24th November, 1458, at the gates of Paris, at Aubervilliers, a small suburb. The copyist's name is known: Pierre Faure or Favre, curé of Aubervilliers and a humble priest. This information is contained in a note by the calligrapher at the end of the manuscript.[1] The actual date of the arrival of the book in Munich is unknown, but there is evidence that in 1628 it belonged to Maximilian the Great, first Elector of Bavaria.[2] Much discussion has arisen over the identity of the person for whom the book was copied. The calligrapher tells us his name in the last three lines of his important note but they are so much defaced as to be illegible.

For a long time the theory was upheld that the commission for the book was made by Etienne Chevalier. The anagrammatical inscription which appears on nine of the miniatures: 'Sur ly n'a Regard': was thought to be the device of the 'trésorier du roi' and the unicorn which appears on the binding and on some of the pages was also considered to refer to the same patron. The conclusion, launched by M. Vallet de Viriville, was that the calligrapher's note at the end of the Munich Boccaccio must have

[1]L'an mil quatre cens cinquante et huit, et le vingtquatriesme jour de Novembre, regnant Charles, VII de ce nom, par la grace de Dieu roy de France, l'an de son règne le xxxvjᵉ, fut accompli de copier et transcire ce présent livre de Bocace cy dessus intitulé, au lieu de Haubervillier-lez-Saint Denis-en-France, par moy Pierre Faure, humble presbtre et serviteur de Dieu, et curé dudict lieu pour et au prouffit de honnourable homme et saige maistre . . . .

[2]An inventory of Maximilian's works of art reads: 'Ein auf pergament geschriebenes Buech in folio, genannt: Joannes Boccatius, Histoire des Nobles Hommes et Femmes, mit villen gross und klainen sauber gemalten Historien; ist in roth mit golt getruckhtes Leder und 2 vergulten Clausuren eingebundten'.

N.B.—The same binding is still on the book, including the two original clasps.

finished with the words: '. . . saige maistre Etienne Chevalier, maistre des comptes et trésorier général du roy, nostre sire'.

This theory became so widely accepted that it was forgotten that M. de Viriville's reconstruction of the last lines was merely an ingenious flight of imagination and his theory came to be considered as actual fact. An authority so distinguished as Monsieur Saint-René-Taillandier declared, in the *Revue des Deux Mondes*, that the manuscript was copied for Etienne Chevalier 'comme l'indique la dernière ligne du texte'.

The connection, however, of Etienne Chevalier with the Munich Boccaccio was entirely specious and it remained for Comte Durrieu, the Sherlock Holmes amongst scholarly research workers, to explode the theory and to expound the problem's true solution. Comte Durrieu disposes of the argument step by step. He points out that the unicorns on the binding of the Munich Boccaccio and in the text have no heraldic significance but are a purely conventional ornament much in evidence at the time. Decorations of *flora* and *fauna* were the constant resource of the tactful artist, for he knew that a sprinkling of elaborate flowers and weird beasts throughout the pages would be certain to please. Moreover, even if the unicorn were part of Etienne Chevalier's heraldic code, it was a decoration which he never used; the only device which he used was his initial letters, bound together with a knotted *lacs* or *cordon*.

As regards the inscription, Comte Durrieu is equally emphatic. The upholders of the Chevalier theory had considered that the constant repetition of 'Sur ly n'a Regard' indicated the connection of the Boccaccio Manuscript with Etienne Chevalier[1] and they disregarded the fact that the inscription was frequently accompanied by the initials LG, which could have nothing at all to do with the King's Treasurer.

---

[1] A French author of the time of Louis XIV Denys Godefroi in his history of Charles VII (1661) claims to have seen on the door of a house in the Rue de la Verrerie, which once belonged to Etienne Chevalier, the words: RIEN SUR LY N'A REGAR.

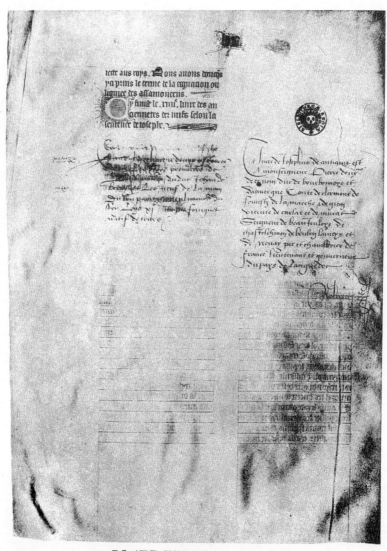

PLATE XXXVI (*see page* 99)
ROBERTET'S NOTES AT THE END OF VOL. I OF
THE *ANTIQUITÉS JUDAÏQUES*
Paris: Bibliothèque Nationale (MS. fr. 247)
[*to face page* 87]

By a process of minute deduction and by the examination of the calligrapher's note in every sort of light, natural and artificial, Comte Durrieu discovered that the last line contained the word 'Laurens', and found, moreover, references to 'la recette générale des finances' and to the 'notaire; secrétaire du roi'. This step being gained, he realized that the inscription, if it referred to some functionary or financial official of not sufficiently dignified rank to possess a device, might well be an anagram and readily applied it to the text. After much manipulation, the solution appeared in the name Laurens Gyrard, who was financial administrator to the Crown in 1458.

Faure's puzzling inscription then would read: 'Saige maistre, Laurens Gyrard, notaire et secrétaire du roy nostre sire et contrerolleur de la recette générale de ses finances'.

The treatise of Boccaccio, *Des Cas des Nobles Hommes et Femmes Malheureux* (*De Casibus Virorum et Mulierum Illustrium*), was more serious than the Decameron, but it achieved a remarkable success throughout the Middle Ages. This review of the sufferings and complaints of the most famous unfortunates of ancient times (Adam and Eve, Samson, Dido, Saul, Mithridates, etc.) was written with a distinctly moral aim, and the clues to its argument were such well-worn clichés as the dangers of disobedience, the vicissitudes of fortune and the perfidy of women. *De Casibus* was read continually for nigh upon two hundred years; Charles d'Orléans was particularly fond of it and chose it as the book with which to while away his time when a prisoner in England.

The translation of the Latin original into French, executed by Laurent de Premierfait under the auspices of the Duc de Berry, made an instant impression and was read all over France. The translator, being a man of scholarship and with knowledge of the world, amplified and embellished Boccaccio's original by the fruits of his own experience and transformed the book from a reiteration of moral problems into a nutshell history of social developments from Adam and Eve until the fourteenth century.

Premierfait's translation was dedicated to the greatest bibliophile of the day (and one of the greatest of all time), the Duc de Berry, and, according to custom, the translator offered the first copy of the new version to the Duc. There is evidence that the Duc de Berry accepted another copy of the same work as a present from the Bishop of Chartres and Monsieur Durrieu considers that this copy is now in the Library of Geneva.

The news of Premierfait's success spread quickly and copies were swiftly made; among the well-known people who possessed the work were Jacques d'Armagnac, Jehan Sans Peur, Charles the Bold and many members of the family of Louis XI. It is said, indeed, that Henry VII of England possessed the book.

But to us, this list of Premierfait's distinguished patrons is of little value compared with the fact that a copy was in the possession of the King's controller of finances, the successor of Etienne Chevalier, Laurens Gyrard. To him, indeed, the highest honour and good fortune fell, for it was he alone who possessed a copy of the book to which at least the frontispiece and probably some of the smaller decorations were by our matchless native of Tours.

Most of the copies of Premierfait's version of the Boccaccio allegory were commissioned by people of wealth and distinction and it is safe to suppose that nearly all the copies were adorned with miniatures or painted decorations. The sequence of dramatic occurrences of which the book was composed gave the artist scope for great variety and subtle imagination. The copy of the book which is now at Geneva, and which may have been the second volume in the possession of the Duc de Berry, is profusely illustrated and contains a hundred and forty-four miniatures.

The *Boccace de Munich*, however, is less elaborately illustrated, but the quality is exceptional; the text is divided into nine sections, at the head of each of which is a large miniature; eighty small miniatures adorn the text to mark the head of each new chapter, and a large frontispiece heralds the entire work.

The smaller miniatures which mark the various sections and chapters of the book are all designed in close relation with the contents of the text. Most of them are conceived in continuous

88

PLATE XXXVII (*see page* 105)
THE MARRIAGE OF ADAM AND EVE
'Enlumineur du Duc de Berry': *Antiquités Judaïques*
Paris: Bibliothèque Nationale (MS. fr. 247)
[*to face page* 88]

action, representing in one single space some of the more important incidents in the book. We see, then, in one small painting, the Fate of the Three Cleopatras or, in another, the Story of Œdipus from the incident of his birth to the marriage with his mother.

The interest of these small paintings is great and their significance is both learned and intricate. Each incident which they portray refers intimately to the text and an understanding of the artist's allusions demands a knowledge of the book's contents.

The quality of the painting is exceptionally refined and the proportions are at times so microscopic that a magnifying glass is necessary for appreciation of the detail. Incidents such as the masons building Carthage and the death of Mithridates at the hands of his soldiers are presented on such a miniature scale that even with a glass they are difficult to see.

Whoever may have been the artist from whose hand or at whose inspiration these miniatures came—and who is to say that it was not Foucquet?—he was, without doubt, a man who knew both Italy and France; many of the paintings contain views of Rome and glimpses of such well-known buildings as Trajan's Column, the Castello di S. Angelo and the Pantheon are by no means rare. As in the *Hours of Etienne Chevalier,* there is a delicious mixture of Gothic and Renaissance elements, and, intermingled with the little French houses with their gables, slates and weather-cocks, we see, on occasion, medallions, pilasters, columns and triumphal arches, which tell the story of another fashion from beyond the Alps.

But, more surprising than these small miniatures, is the large and famous frontispiece, known as the 'Lit de Vendôme', by which they are preceded (Plate I). This page is peculiar to the Munich volume and does not occur in any other copy of *Des Cas des Nobles Hommes et Femmes Malheureux.* This subject has no relation to the text or to the author, but represents a contemporary event—an incident which was stirring the whole of France whilst the book was being copied for Laurens Gyrard. Monsieur Vallet de Viriville was the first to identify the subject of this page, recognizing it to be the 'Lit de Justice' or Solemn Assembly of Justice held at Vendôme in 1458 under the King of France, Charles VII, in which the sentence of death was passed upon Jehan, Duc d'Alençon, a prince of the royal blood and one of the most wealthy and respected men in France. The idea of setting this dramatic incident at the head of *Des Cas des Nobles Hommes et Femmes Malheureux* was one which only a great artist could conceive or properly carry out, and the marvellous skill with which the scheme has been put into practice recalls one artist and one only, Jehan Foucquet of Tours.

It must at once be admitted that, both in style, technique and colour, this great frontispiece is vastly superior to the smaller miniatures in the book, but this distinction does not rule out the possibility of Foucquet's rôle in the decoration of the manuscript. The smaller miniatures are, undoubtedly, unequal in quality but most of those which mark the separate divisions are of a quality sufficiently excellent to make the theory of the hand of Foucquet not impossible. In these paintings, many of the elements in which Foucquet excelled appear: a marvellous ingenuity in the grouping of the masses; a delicate attempt at local colour; a purity of colouring and an accuracy of perspective which at times are unsurpassed; and a feeling for landscape—with delicious vistas over sun-reflecting watercourses and expanses of green fields which can be reminiscent only of our painter.

Certain of the eighty very small miniatures which appear amongst the text reveal a feeble hand, but this can surely be taken as a sign of the work of master and pupil. The book contains an artistic unity which indicates that it was inspired by one master artist and executed in part by some less skilled pupil. If Raphael and Rubens allowed their disciples scope and license, where then is the impossibility of similar generosity on the part of our artist of Tours?

The theory of Foucquet's authorship is considerably recent in date. In the past, many suggestions—some very fantastic—have been raised. At one time it was thought that Jan van Eyck

PLATE XXXVIII (see page 106)
THE STORY OF JOSEPH
'Enlumineur du Duc de Berry': *Antiquités Judaïques*
Paris: Bibliothèque Nationale (MS. fr. 247)
[*to face page 90*]

painted the 'Lit de Vendôme' and at another a ludicrous confusion was made which led to the supposition that Pierre Faure (the calligrapher and modest curé of Aubervilliers) was the artist of the frontispiece.

The first scholars to regard the manuscript in the light of Foucquet were Waagen and the Comte de Laborde, and they both saw in it much affinity with the *Hours of Etienne Chevalier* at Chantilly. At once they recognized its undeniable points of similarity both in the types of faces portrayed, the poises of the figures, the landscape backgrounds and the mixture of architectural styles. But the researches of these learned gentlemen went only half the way and it remained for the Comte Durrieu to compare the manuscript, not with the Chantilly Hours (which, after all, have never definitely been authenticated to Foucquet) but with the one manuscript of which Foucquet's authorship is certain, the *Antiquités Judaïques*.

Comte Durrieu at once noted that the four salient characteristics of the *Antiquités Judaïques* are also those of the Munich Boccaccio: a sense of scientific composition; a predilection for animated battle scenes; the radiant representation of nature; and the marvellous judgment of the values of light and perspective.

Each one of these qualities can be confirmed by a comparison of the two works, and an examination of the detail in both the manuscripts strengthens the theory of their analogy. The figures of workmen and warriors, horses, chariots, and all the trappings of military expeditions; the sense of architecture and the passion for colours which resemble sheets of liquid light—all these elements are similar and are equally dominant in one manuscript as in the other. The Italian influence, moreover, is present in one work as in the other and both the books are incontestably the product of a man who has visited Italy.

The Munich manuscript was copied in November 1458, the year of the famous trial which lasted from August till October and which was conducted always in the presence of the King. The prisoner was the Duc d'Alençon and the charge high treason. The Duc was accused of having conspired with the English against the interests of his own country. On the 10th October, 1458, the Duc was deprived of all his goods and estates and the sentence of death was passed upon him. It is not, indeed, difficult to imagine that the trial at Vendôme was the burning topic at the time when the manuscript was being copied; its representation, therefore, by the artist as an example of a veritable 'cas d'un noble homme' indicates a vivid agility of mind and a swift sense of the poignant and dramatic which only the greatest possess.

The scene of Foucquet's famous frontispiece is laid in the interior of a vast hall, in the middle of which is a lozenge-shaped enclosure. The walls of the hall are hung with tapestries of alternate bands of red, white and green, the colours of Charles VII. The design of the tapestry is the rose plant, another royal emblem. On either side, across the tapestries, are two winged stags with a crown around their necks, the device of Charles VII, adopted from his father, Charles VI, through his grandfather, Charles V. The wooden balustrade, which forms the court, and the throne on which the King presides are covered with a stuff decorated with a design of golden fleur-de-lys on a blue ground. On the floor of the court is a carpet of the same design which, according to a contemporary authority, suffered so greatly from the continual passing of feet during the four months of the trial that it had to be drastically repaired.

The artist has depicted the scene at the dramatic moment when the verdict is about to be given; beyond the barrier, the crowd, despite the efforts of the guards to restrain them, eagerly press forward to catch each word of the trial's result. Within the court the speeches are over; the accused has retired and the sentence is being read by the criminal bailiff Hughes Alligret who stands, book in hand, facing the Chancellor.

The scene is portrayed with such a sensitive refinement that the identities of all the most distinguished assistants at the trial can be traced. On the King's left, the highest seats are occupied by the Peers of the French Church; among them can be seen the Archbishop of Rheims, Jehan Jouvenel des Ursins, brother of the Chancellor; the Bishops of Laon, Paris, Beauvais and Châlons, and the Abbé of Saint Denis, Philippe de Gamaches, who sits on the extreme end of the bench, near the door, clothed in the severe habit of the Benedictines. Beneath the prelates sit the laymen, such as the Seigneur de la Tour d'Auvergne, Jehan Bureau, trésorier de France, and other distinguished folk. On the bench, back to the spectators, sit the high civil functionaries such as Tristan l'Hermite and Etienne Chevalier.

The mastery with which the groups are managed and the extraordinary perception with which the artist has portrayed the crowd immediately suggest the hand of Foucquet and of none other. The aspect and expressions of the people who throng against the enclosure and press against the guards give us a glimpse of life itself. Most of the costumes are French, but there is one man in the crowd who wears a kind of Florentine headdress, whilst another is bearded and wears an Eastern turban. Every member of the crowd has the interest and significance of an individual portrait. Especially remarkable is the old man in the left foreground with the ermine cap: this figure might almost be a portrait by Van Eyck and, in its robust conviviality, it also anticipates a famous figure in English painting of over three hundred years later: the monk in Hogarth's Calais Gate.

On the extreme right of the picture, with his head touching the border, is a young man who seems impervious to the developments of the trial and takes no part in the excitement. It seems by no means unlikely that this is a self-portrait of our artist; its similarity to the Louvre enamel is certainly very striking, and, in including himself among the crowd, Foucquet would be fulfilling a caprice to which even Raphael once fell a victim.

CHAPTER NINE

FOUCQUET AND JOSEPHUS

(a) The History of the Manuscript of the Antiquités Judaïques

THE COMBINATION of these two famous names has a far-reaching significance, since it is in Foucquet's connection with Josephus that the corner-stone of the argument which we have built around the artist is to be found. The marvellous manuscript of the *Antiquités Judaïques* is the only work in which the hand of Foucquet is definitely authenticated; for this fact alone its interest is incomparable and a history of its entire existence is not out of place.

Flavius Josephus was born in Jerusalem about September A.D. 37 and belonged to a family of Jewish priests. His life was one of great variety and adventure; in his early years he went to Rome, under the reign of Nero, to beg grace for some unjustly persecuted compatriots and he returned to his native land at the time of the Jewish rebellion against the Roman rule. Throughout his life Josephus admired Rome and its prestige and, although a member of a subordinate and inimical people, he won the favour of Vespasian, under whose patronage he went again to Rome, where he lived until his death. Josephus, indeed, enjoyed imperial favour under three reigns: those of Vespasian, Titus and Domitian; and it was in the Imperial City that he died, towards the year A.D. 100 or perhaps a little later.

Josephus's principal claim to remembrance lies in his writings and, especially, in his two most famous works: the *De Antiquitatibus Judaeorum* (a History of the Jewish People from the Creation of the World to the declaration of War with Rome in A.D. 66) and the *War of the Jews against the Romans*. The latter work is,

PLATE XXXIX (*see page* 113)
THE DOWNFALL OF KORAH, DATHAN AND ABIRON
Antiquités Judaïques
Paris: Bibliothèque Nationale (MS. fr. 247)
[*to face page* 95]

perhaps, more interesting than the former, since the events which the author describes are more recent and not infrequently are incidents of which he had himself been an eye-witness.

Of all the writers of antiquity, Josephus was the most fashionable in the Middle Ages and his books, which told of a time so near the age of Christ, were regarded almost as *Histoires Saintes*. Josephus, himself, transcribed his works into Greek, but it was not until the sixth century that, under the order of Cassiodorus, they were translated into Latin. From this Latin translation both of the two most famous works were constantly copied during the Middle Ages and they were frequently combined in one volume, the one treatise following the other. As a mark of the extreme interest taken in Josephus's work, it is, perhaps, interesting to note that the British Museum possesses twenty manuscripts of these two books, both fragmentary and complete, dating from the eleventh to the fifteenth centuries. The craze for Josephus continued until after the year 1500, for it was at the beginning of the sixteenth century that the Cardinal Georges d'Amboise commissioned a magnificent copy of the *De Antiquitatibus Judaeorum*, decorated with every variety of miniature and illumination.[1]

The demand for the two treatises upon the Jewish people was so great that the Latin translation was far from being an adequate supply and the work was quickly translated into French. Under the reign of Charles VI, we hear of an anonymous translation of the two works, called by the comprehensive title: *Les Anciennetés des Juifs selon Josèphe*. Other adaptations followed suit.

With the invention of printing, the works of the Jewish historian were more widely popularized; in December 1492 Antoine Vérard, a bookseller, published under the title of *La Bataille Judaïque* a new translation of the *War of the Jews against the Romans*. This translation is sometimes attributed to Claude de Seyssel. From all accounts, Vérard's publication was a handsome

---

[1] The book was still in demand even in the seventeenth century, when the translation of Arnauld d'Andilly (published in Paris in 1667) achieved an enormous vogue.

achievement, and the Bibliothèque Nationale possesses a magnificent copy on vellum offered by the editor to Charles VIII.

It is with the earlier French version—the anonymously compiled *Anciennetés des Juifs selon Josèphe*—that we must here concern ourselves. The circumstances concerning the distribution of this version have only partly been made manifest but a few facts are certain: a copy was sent in January 1410 to the royal library of the Louvre by the Duc de Guyenne, the King's son, and at about the same time (and certainly not later than 1413) two other copies were in the hands of the Duc de Berry, brother of Charles V. The Duc was a man of versatile capacities and his life was divided between the exercising of a suspicious and crafty form of government and the collection of supreme works of art. As a bibliophile he was unsurpassed and in his many residences (at Paris, Poitiers, Bourges and Riom) he possessed a collection of precious books which few French—and indeed European—collectors could equal. As a patron of the arts the Duc was supremely influential and he welcomed every sort of artist, whether painter, sculptor, architect, engraver, or master in wrought iron. This great Mecænas of the arts was not, indeed, a mere figurehead or plutocrat collector; for him each treasure had its cachet and each book in his collection possessed its special interest. In each volume he wrote his name and inscribed critical notes in the margins.

Among the precious manuscripts of the Duc de Berry, there were three copies of the treatises of Josephus, one of which was a Latin translation and the other two were copies of the anonymous *Anciennetés*. Of the latter two, the first is a handsome volume, illustrated with one large miniature and twenty-five small ones, which is now in the Bibliothèque Nationale;[1] and the second is the famous volume which makes the subject of this chapter.

The manuscript of the *Antiquités Judaïques,* to which we here refer, was from the beginning divided into two volumes, both

[1] MS. fr. 6446. After the death of the Duc de Berry, it belonged to his nephew, the Duc de Bourgogne (Jehan Sans Peur), who was assassinated in 1419. Later the manuscript found its way to Brussels, where it long remained.

PLATE XL (*see page* 114)
THE SIEGE OF JERICHO
Antiquités Judaïques
Paris: Bibliothèque Nationale (MS. fr. 247)
[*to face page* 97]

of which after many wanderings are now reunited in the Bibliothèque Nationale.

There are many proofs that these volumes of Josephus's treatise were once in the possession of the Duc de Berry: in Volume I, at the bottom of the third folio and at the foot of the first large illustration, is a representation of the Duc's arms; in the third miniature of the same volume, on the pennons which surmount the Hebrews' tents, is seen the blazon of the Duc; and further evidence of the Duc's ownership is given in the librarian's note, the significance of which will be discussed later. Volume II, moreover, bears equally indisputable signs of the Duc's possession: on the first page is the Duc de Berry's autograph, *Jehan*; and on the last page are two notes written by the same hand.[1]

Examination of the manuscript reveals a further stage in the history of its existence, and there is evidence to show that the two volumes became, at a later date, the property of the great-grandson of the Duc de Berry: Jacques d'Armagnac, Duc de Nemours and Comte de la Marche. A definite proof of this second ownership is found at the end of the first volume in the autographical note: 'Ce premier volume de Josèphe est au Duc de Nemours—Jacques'. The first large miniature, moreover, in this volume is surmounted by the arms of the Duc Jacques: two syrens, the traditional device of the House of Armagnac; and on a scroll brandished by a young woman on the border is seen the family motto of the Duc Jacques: FORTUNE D'AMIS. These words frequently occur throughout the manuscript.

In the second volume, on the reverse side of the last page of the text, is another autograph of the Duc Jacques written underneath the second note by the Duc Jehan de Berry.[2] The Duc Jacques, moreover, was accustomed to inscribe in each of his books the

---

[1](*a*) Ce livre est au duc de Berry.—Jehan.

  Ce livre de Josèphe est au duc de Berry.—Jehan.

[2]Ce livre de Josèphe est au duc de Berry.—Jehan.

  Et de présant *à* son fils (*i.e.* direct descendant) le duc de Nemouz et Comte de la Marche—Jaques—Pour Carlat.

number of pages and miniatures (*ystoires*) which the volume contained; and on the reverse side of the last page of the second volume we find the note: 'En ce livre a III^c IIII feuilles et XIII histoires'.

Much conjecture has arisen as to the means by which the manuscript passed from the possession of the Duc de Berry to that of his great-grandson. The evidence of inventories and the many deductions which may be drawn from documents of this kind have testified that the manuscript of the *Antiquités Judaïques* was acquired by the Duc de Berry in or about 1403 and passed out of his collection about the year 1413, three years before his death. Now the Duc was very generous in the giving away of his treasures and had, on more than one occasion, presented his kinsmen with precious books, so that it is not unreasonable to suppose that this copy of Josephus was given to a member of the Armagnac family whom he held in high regard.

There need be little regret that such a precious book left the possession of the Duc de Berry, for the Duc de Nemours et d'Armagnac was as passionate a bibliophile as his great-grandfather had been and inherited all his tastes as a collector. Like his distinguished ancestor, the Duc Jacques inscribed his name in books and made reflective critical notes; he also added an indication of the residence to which the book was destined: 'pour la Marche, pour Castres, ou pour Carlat'. The second volume of our Josephus bears the note 'pour Carlat'.

The Duc d'Armagnac, as bibliophile, was as princely as he was enthusiastic, and commissioned magnificently decorated books; he took interest, moreover, in ancient manuscripts and had their pages restored and their binding repaired. He employed, too, craftsmen of the highest skill, such as Evrard d'Espinques (a French artist of German origin), Maistre Guillaume Alexandre of Paris, and Maistre Jehan Foucquet of Tours.

The Duc had a tragic destiny: four years after his accession to the dukedom of Nemours (1461), he joined the *Ligue du Bien Public*, making thereby a fatal *volte-face*, which, despite a temporary reconciliation with the King, finally brought about his imprisonment in

PLATE XLI (*see page* 115)
THE DOWNFALL OF THE SONS OF ELI
Antiquités Judaïques
Paris: Bibliothèque Nationale (MS. fr. 247)
[*to face page* 98]

the Dauphiné and, after a period of confinement in the Bastille, his execution in Paris in 1477, 'before an immense and sympathetic crowd'. The story of this hapless prince's downfall has always kept a firm hold in French minds and was the subject of a play, written in the nineteenth century by Casimir de la Vigne.

For the next stage in the history of this famous book we have to refer to the librarian's note at the end of the first volume. On the back of the last page of the text and in the right-hand column, François Robertet, the secretary and librarian of the Duc Pierre de Bourbon, has testified that the volume was in his master's possession.[1] A further proof of this ownership is revealed in the painting over of the arms of Armagnac with the arms of Bourbon and in the fact that the 'fleur de lys' of the Royal House is superimposed upon the 'ear of corn' of the family of Armagnac. Beside his confirmation of the volume's whereabouts Robertet adds another note of even greater interest, assigning three of the miniatures to an artist contemporary with the Duc de Berry and others to our celebrated native of Tours.[2] Robertet's invaluable information must have been written between the years 1488 and 1503, since it was on the first of these dates that Pierre, Sire de Beaujeu, became the Duc de Bourbon, and on the last of them that he died.

The exceptional importance of this first volume of Josephus's treatise, which contains not only miniatures of a miraculous beauty but a note assigning the greater part of them to the 'bon paintre et enlumineur, Jehan Foucquet, natif de Tours', makes a research into

[1]'Ce livre de Josephus, de Antiquis, est à monseigneur Pierre, deuxiesme de ce nom, duc de Bourbonneys et d'Auvergne, conte de Clermont, de Fourestz, de la Marche et de Giem, viconte de Carlat et de Murat, seigneur de Beaujeuloys, de Chastel-Chinon, de Bourbon-Lanceys et de Nonay, per et chamberier de France, lieutenant et gouverneur du pays de Languedoc.'— Robertet.

The Duc Pierre de Bourbon, son-in-law of Louis XI, was chosen by the King to go to Carlat for the arrest of the Duc de Nemours on the charge of treason.

[2]'En ce livre a douze ystoires, les trois premières de l'enlumineur du duc Jehan de Berry et les neuf de la main du bon paintre et enlumineur du roi Louis XI, Jehan Foucquet, natif de Tours' (Plate XXXVI).

the complete history of the book's vagaries highly desirable. Up
to the present stage we have seen that both the volumes passed
from the possession of the Duc de Berry into the library of the
Duc de Nemours, and that later the first volume[1] found its way
into the ownership of Pierre, Duc de Bourbon. There is evidence
that the volume of the *Antiquités Judaïques* was not the only book
which Pierre possessed from the collection of the Duc de Nemours, since inventories tell us that his library contained other
volumes which had once been possessed by the unfortunate
Jacques d'Armagnac. The problem then arises as to the reason of
this change, and the events which led to the acquisition of these
precious books by the Duc de Bourbon have been the pivot of
much conjecture.

Comte Durrieu, in his great monograph on the *Antiquités
Judaïques*, has based a theory upon four distinct hypotheses.

First, he suggests that the order for arrest on 10th July, 1477,
against Jacques d'Armagnac, Duc de Nemours, adjudicated all
the goods and possessions of the condemned into the favour of
the King. In a letter dated 10th August, Louis XI declares that
all the goods 'meubles ou immeubles' of Jacques d'Armagnac
were 'lui advenus comme confisqués'. If this were truly the case,
the King might well have left the book to his daughter Anne de
Beaujeu, who became the wife of Pierre, Duc de Bourbon.

Secondly, Durrieu raises the supposition that the volume was
sold to the Duc de Bourbon with the Duc de Nemours' library
and possessions. We know from the owner's note in the volume
that the book was destined for Carlat, and it is historically established that, during the trial, the viscounty of·Carlat was remitted
to the Crown, although it was restored to Jacques' son, Jehan
d'Armagnac, at a later date. In 1489, Jehan d'Armagnac sold the
castles of Carlat and Murat to the Duc Pierre de Bourbon, and,
according to Paulin Paris, part of the library of their former
owner went with the sale.

[1]The history of Vol. II is more mysterious and will be dealt with separately. Cp. p. 103.

Both these first hypotheses seem at once attractive, but, as the Comte Durrieu points out, neither is entirely satisfactory. If the first were true, it is bizarre that Robertet makes no mention of the King's former possession and, as regards the second, there are reasons to believe that the manuscript belonged to Pierre before the sale of the Armagnac castles.[1]

The third suggestion is that Pierre de Bourbon inherited the volume on the death (in 1488) of his brother Jehan, from which date he acceded to the duchy. Jehan, the first Duc de Bourbon, was a bibliophile and had married Catherine d'Armagnac, the daughter of the hapless Jacques. The possibility, then, arises that the possessions of Jacques d'Armagnac were passed on to his daughter, Catherine, and later to her husband and, thence, to his brother Pierre. This hypothesis, however, is shaken by the fact that several volumes from the library of Jacques d'Armagnac seem to have been in Pierre's possession before the death of his brother Jehan.

The fourth—and most probable—hypothesis is that the precious volume entered Pierre's possession through a far less honourable means than those already suggested. When Pierre was ordered by Louis XI to arrest Jacques d'Armagnac in the castle of Carlat, he was accompanied and seconded by Tannegui du Châtel, vicomte de la Bellière, and by Jehan du Mas, seigneur de l'Asle. Now, it is known that among the manuscripts in Jacques' possession some became the property of Pierre's two accomplices, and it seems only natural to suppose that their leader should have chosen the best share of the pillage for himself and have selected the greater and most precious part of the library. Comte Durrieu, therefore, is of the opinion that the first volume of the Josephus passed straight into the hands of Pierre de Bourbon as booty from the estate of Armagnac.

The further stages in the history of the first volume are far less

---

[1]An examination of the heraldic devices of certain other volumes possessed by the Duc de Bourbon and which came from the Duc d'Armagnac reveal evidences of their having entered his possession in 1488.

complicated. Pierre de Bourbon died in 1503 and his possessions went to his only heir, his daughter, Suzanne, who married Charles de Bourbon, Comte de Montpensier and the famous 'Connétable de France'. After the revolt of Charles against the King, Francis I, in 1522 and his condemnation as a traitor, his goods were remitted to the Crown and, with them, the first volume of Josephus. An inventory of the books belonging to the Connétable de Bourbon which the King had removed from his library at Moulins to his own library at Blois or Fontainebleau[1] shows that among them were three volumes of Josephus's work: a translation into Latin, an historical compilation and a translation into French.[2] Of these three the first two do not concern us, but the last is, with little doubt, the volume containing the miniatures by our 'Natif de Tours'.

From Blois or Fontainebleau, the books went to Paris; in a catalogue of the royal library of 1622, we find an undoubted reference to our book (14 livres de l'Antiquité de Josèphe en Français). From the royal possession the volumes—and Foucquet's miniatures among them—found their way into the Bibliothèque Nationale.[3]

[1]It is not certain to which of these royal residences the Josephus volume went. In an inventory of 1560 of the books at Fontainebleau, there is a reference to a copy of the *Anciennetés des Juifs*, which may have been the first volume of our manuscript.

[2]Le livre de Josephus, en françois a deux fermaus d'argent doré.

[3]Genealogical sequence of the history of the first volume of the *Antiquités Judaïques*:

Duc de Berry
|
Jacques d' Armagnac, Duc de Nemours
|
Pierre, Duc de Bourbon
|
Suzanne, Comtesse de Montpensier
|
Louis XI
|
Royal Library, Paris
|
Bibliothèque Nationale

PLATE XLII (*see page* 115)
DAVID LAMENTING OVER THE DEATH OF SAUL
Antiquités Judaïques
Paris: Bibliothèque Nationale (MS. fr. 247)

[*to face page* 103]

FOUCQUET AND JOSEPHUS

The entire history of the first volume of the *Antiquités Judaïques* has, therefore, been traced, but, with the second volume, greater problems arise. It is evident that the two volumes were separated at an early date; both of them were in the possession of the Duc de Berry and his great-grandson, Jacques d'Armagnac, but there is no trace of the second volume after the démise of the latter owner. Nothing but complete mystification ensues after the dissolution of the goods at Carlat; there is no trace that the second volume passed into the possession of the Duc de Bourbon and there is no mention of it in the inventory of the library at Moulins.

The disappearance, therefore, of the second volume was intimately concerned with the downfall of Jacques d'Armagnac but the circumstances are entirely unknown and it is not until the eighteenth century that there is news of it again. This time the scene is changed from France to England, since an inscription in the book itself tells us that in 1750 (perhaps 56) the volume was in London in the library of a certain Mr. Palmer. In 1814, the book appeared again as No. 888 in the catalogue of the Towneley sale, and then, comet-like, it vanished for another ninety years. In 1903, it figured once more in a sale catalogue and was recognized by the purchaser, the late Mr. Yates Thompson, as the second volume of the Josephus which had once belonged to the Duc de Berry. Its condition, however, had changed since the sale of 1814; at that time it was embellished with thirteen miniatures and now it had only one. A hue and cry was raised after the missing twelve; ten of them were found in the royal library at Windsor, but the remaining two have never been discovered. King Edward VII, with characteristic graciousness and respect for things French, considered that the book should be united to its companion volume. With the acquiescence of Mr. Yates Thompson, he had the ten loose leaves reintegrated into the main volume and went, in person, to Paris to present the book to the President of the French Republic.[1]

[1] 4th March, 1906.

103

It is, then, a romantic history which has befallen these two precious volumes. After many wanderings and much adversity they have found their way back to the country from which they came, and the only desire which now remains is that if the two missing leaves are ever found the discovery will be made by someone who will, like the two English owners, think fit to restore the volumes in the Bibliothèque Nationale to their pristine completeness.

The study of the miniatures in the two volumes of Josephus's *Antiquités Judaïques* must be tripartal, since at least three distinct hands were responsible for their making, The first three miniatures in the first volume are, according to Robertet's note, the work of the 'Enlumineur du Duc Jehan de Berry'; the remaining pages in this volume and the first large miniature of the second are the undoubted work of Jehan Foucquet; whereas the small miniatures in Volume II are the creations of yet another hand. It remains, therefore, to make a critical examination of each of these three sets and to expose the theories which most scholars, and particularly the Comte Durrieu, have launched concerning the identification of the 'ducal illuminator' and the artist of the second volume.

(b) The 'Enlumineur du Duc de Berry'

'En ce livre a douze ystoires, les trois premières (sont) de l'enlumineur du Duc Jehan de Berry.' So speaks Robertet with wisdom, and it is by this dictum that we must abide.

The first example of painting in the volume, however, is not a full-sized miniature (*ystoire*), but a little picture in the inside of the initial letter C in a space which the calligrapher has reserved at the head of the prologue. This painting, now worn almost beyond recognition, represents an author sitting at a desk and consulting books ranged around him on a revolving stand.[1] The

[1] A similar stand occurs in a miniature in the Book of Hours from the Holford Collection, of which at least two pages seem to be by Foucquet himself.

PLATE XLIII (see page 116)
THE BUILDING OF THE TEMPLE
Antiquités Judaïques
Paris: Bibliothèque Nationale (MS. fr. 247)
[*to face page* 104]

author wears a long gilded gown and a little red and gold cap of a conical shape such as was fashionable in—and indeed unknown until—the time of Charles VII and Louis XI. This, therefore, post-dates the painting to a period later than the Duc de Berry and makes it impossible to suppose that it represents the work of the Duc's *enlumineur*. Whether Foucquet, himself, was the artist of this tiny painting is difficult to determine owing to the bad condition into which the pigments have relapsed, but the problem is not one of great importance. The painting may be Foucquet's work, or may be that of an imitator; it might even be taken as the work of the artist of the ten small miniatures in the second volume.

The first large miniature in the *Antiquités Judaïques* and the initial example of the work of the 'enlumineur du Duc Jehan de Berry' represents the 'Marriage of Adam and Eve by the Almighty in the Earthly Paradise' (Plate XXXVII), The Deity, clad in a golden robe, protects the couple with His cloak, of which two angels support the upper edges. The Paradise is inhabited by many different animals, including two bears, sheep, deer, rabbits, a lion and a porcupine. A wall, flanked with castellated turrets, encloses the garden and separates it from a river in which are swans and an abundance of fish.

The upper half of the picture is circumscribed by a kind of rainbow bearing the first six signs of the Zodiac and above it, in a small tympanum, is another representation of God, blessing with His right hand, and in His left holding the architect's compasses, which embrace the sun. Behind the Deity, in a glory, are cherubim and on either side are angels bearing a drill and hammer, the instruments of work. Above on the marginal framework are two angels; the one holding an instrument for raising stones and the other holding a set square.

On the border, at the sides and on the base, are the arms and other signs of the ownership of Jacques d'Armagnac to which a reference has already been made.[1]

The style of this miniature is distinctly archaic, with its con-

[1]Cp. p. 97.

ventionalized arrangement of the masses and the elementary conception of perspective planes, and there is no doubt at all that it dates from a period preceding that of Jehan Foucquet: the period, indeed, of the Duc de Berry, There are, however, signs that a later hand has been at work upon the painting; the drawing of the faces of Adam and Eve, the head of God and the faces of the angels all suggest a later date than 1416. The head of Eve, indeed, is very unlike most of the female heads of contemporary paintings, and anticipates—if not recalls—the periods of Charles VII and Louis XI. But these hybrid influences in this curious page are not entirely perplexing, for the miniature has evidently been restored at a later date. These additions were in all probability made at the request of Jacques d'Armagnac, for the figures of women in the margin who bear the ducal pennons and the armorial device at the base (both of which are obvious additions) show many points in common with the more recent passages of the main miniature. Such additions, made at the instigation of a new owner who wished to efface signs of previous possession, were by no means rare, and in the case of this miniature they have been executed with taste and skill.

The second miniature, which illustrates Chapters II and III of the text, represents the 'Story of Joseph and the Sons of Jacob' (Plate XXXVIII). In the true mediaeval fashion, the picture is arranged episodically and the scene is set in continuous action. In the upper part of the picture we see Joseph's brothers, clothed in brilliant raiment (rose, blue, green, mauve, vermilion), sitting in the countryside, guarding their flocks. Further to the left, a woman, dressed in blue, is coming out of a kind of castle and bids the young Joseph (traditionally clad in a green tunic) to find his brothers and take them their provisions. In the foreground, the action becomes more agitated; on the left, Joseph is being cast into the well and on the right, the merchants, with their caravan from Gilead, are taking Joseph away and completing the brothers' infamous bargain.

PLATE XLIV (*see page* 117)
SALMANAZAR LEADING INTO CAPTIVITY THE TEN
TRIBES OF EGYPT
Antiquités Judaïques
Paris: Bibliothèque Nationale (MS. fr. 247)
[*to face page* 106]

In this miniature the painter has obviously been in search of local colour. The figures are dressed in Oriental costumes; the types, too, are definitely Eastern, and one of the merchants is a real negro. The strip of water, moreover, near which the incidents are taking place represents the Red Sea and is painted in a deep red tone!

This second miniature differs from its immediate predecessor in that it bears no sign of restoration nor of any introduction of arms or emblems. There is, however, no doubt that it is the work of the same artist as the 'Marriage of Adam and Eve' and the significant qualities of the one can be found with equal clarity in the other.

The third miniature, and last of the series from the brush of the ducal illuminator, represents the 'Hebrews in the Desert after the Exodus from Egypt'. Again the scene is set in episodic form. In the background is the Red Sea, portrayed in the colour of its name as in the preceding miniature, whilst a little further forward is the episode of the Israelites camping in the desert and digging wells which they find filled with bitter waters. Here, the Hebrews' tents deserve notice, since each is surmounted by an armorial pennon bearing the arms of the Duc de Berry.

In the foreground two distinct incidents are portrayed side by side; on the left, the Hebrews are on their knees before the tabernacle containing the Tables of The Law and on the right, amidst a crowd of people, are the five Amalekite Kings, who endeavoured to enlist the favour of the country's population and to induce them to fight with them against the Hebrews. Here, as in the preceding miniature, the artist displays a definite feeling for the East; all the Kings are mounted upon camels and the types which they reveal are realistically Oriental. One of them is definitely Mongolian in appearance; another wears pigtails in Chinese fashion, whilst yet another has a long over-hanging moustache. Their costumes, moreover, are highly spectacular and reflect a tendency towards a conscious Orientalism on the part of the artist.

As in the former miniature, the artist reveals a feeling for animal life. In front of the Amalekite Kings are two dogs, drawn with consummate skill; on a mountain peak in the background an eagle, whose wings are lit by the sun's rays, is devouring its prey; whilst further towards the right, two bears are wandering upon a rock. On the extreme right, a goat is hanging from a tree; this may be a representation of the scapegoat, whose story is told in the third chapter of the Antiquities to which this miniature is a frontispiece. Swans are flying in the sky.

The miniature of the 'Hebrews in the Desert' was certainly executed for the Duc de Berry, since his blazon is seen on the pennons of the encampment. The style, moreover, as in the two preceding pages, is redolent of the early fifteenth century. It has the episodic form and continuous action; the clear-cut design suggestive of a bas-relief; the close observation of nature and the almost naïve insistence upon local colour in costumes and scenery, all of which qualities indicate the period immediately preceding that of Jehan Foucquet, and which date the miniatures to a year not later than 1416, that of the Duc de Berry's death.

The problem now arises as to the identity of the 'enlumineur du Duc de Berry', from whose hand these three fine miniatures came, and here, as before, for the most illuminating solution of the mystery we have to repair to the Comte Durrieu. In his monograph on the *Antiquités Judaïques*, Durrieu has launched a theory for the authorship of these paintings which is so attractive and ingenious that its argument should here be given in full.[1] Robertet, in his note, declares that the first three miniatures are the work of the Duc de Berry's *enlumineur* but his statement is entirely unqualified by any particularization. It is not, then, apparent whether he is speaking in the strict sense of one of the Duc's special illuminators or whether, in a more general sense,[2] he

[1]Comte Durrieu presents his theory only as an hypothesis and not as an incontestable doctrine. He modestly remarks: 'La théorie est séduisante . . . elle ne constitue qu'une hypothèse; et, si je me risque à l'indiquer, ce n'est que sous les plus expresses réserves et presque à titre de rêverie'.

[2]Robertet was writing sixty years after the Duke's death and his memory may well have become a little hazy.

refers to an artist employed by the Duc de Berry but not necessarily part of his suite or the official possessor of the title 'enlumineur du Duc'. The Duc de Berry was such an assiduous collector of books and lavish donor of commissions that he employed a large number of illuminators of varying degrees of excellence. Some, indeed, fell short of excellence and certain of the Duc's volumes reveal the work of inferior craftsmen. But our three miniatures are of an exceedingly high standard and their author must, doubtless, have been one of the most prized among the artists in the ducal service and, most possibly, an *enlumineur du Duc*.

Of the Duc's official *enlumineurs* there are several whose names spring to the mind: Jacques Coene, a Fleming, better known as the 'Maître des Heures du Maréchal de Boucicaut'; André Beauneveu, the painter praised by Froissart; Jacquemart de Hesdin; and lastly, the famous Pol de Limbourg and his brothers. Suggestions have been made connecting each of these artists with the execution of our miniatures, but in the first three cases the assumption was unjustified. The master of the peerless 'Hours of the Maréchal de Boucicaut' practised certain undeniable methods in the drawing of the faces which do not appear in the *Antiquités Judaïques*; André Beauneveu,[1] whom Monsieur Delisle recognized as the author of a series of figures (apostles and prophets) in a Franco-Latin Psalter from the library of the Duc de Berry,[2] reveals a style entirely different from that of the master of our first three miniatures; whilst Jacquemart de Hesdin, an artist of supreme sophistication, must also be rejected, for reasons of style, from the argument. There remain, therefore, only Pol de Limbourg and his brothers.

Historical archives have told us that both Pol de Limbourg and his two brothers were 'enlumineurs du Duc de Berry'. Pol,

[1] The name of Beauneveu was first connected with this manuscript in 1853 by the Comte Horace de Viel-Castel, but the discoveries in 1868 by Monsieur Delisle threw the earlier attribution out of account.

[2] MS. fr. 13091 (Bibliothèque Nationale).

himself, bore the title officially, and the brothers worked continually in the ducal service. For some time it was thought that Pol de Limbourg, himself, was the artist of our miniatures, but again the theory was exploded by the scholarship of Monsieur Delisle, whose attribution in 1884 of the *Très Riches Heures*[1]—a manuscript of miraculous beauty and of a quality far superior to the three pages in our Josephus—to Pol de Limbourg made his authorship impossible. But, although the master of the *Très Riches Heures* never touched the miniatures of the Josephus, there are, between the two works, certain incontestable resemblances of landscape, architecture and colouring which, although they point to no identification, betray an undoubted 'air de parenté'. The theory, then, which the Comte Durrieu promotes—almost in a whisper as if too good to be true—is that the first three miniatures in the *Antiquités Judaïques* were painted by the brothers of Pol de Limbourg, and that they were or one of them was (either Maître Jehannequin or Maître Hermand) the 'enlumineur du Duc de Berry', whose mention by Robertet makes his note at once so instructive and so tantalizing.

(c) The rôle of Foucquet

'. . . les trois premières (ystoires sont) de l'enlumineur du duc de Berry et les neuf de la main du bon paintre et enlumineur du roi Louis XI, Jehan Foucquet, natif de Tours.' This concluding portion of Robertet's statement is of unique value since it pins the authorship of the finest miniatures which the volume contains to our great Tourangeau painter, but, like most other points which concern our artist, it harbours a mystery which none has yet been able definitely to solve. Robertet clearly states that the first volume contains twelve miniatures, three by the ducal illuminator and nine by the native of Tours. But, in reality, the number which the book contains is fourteen. What, then, is the reason for the librarian's inaccuracy? Various suggestions have been made and all are possible. It is conceivable that, at the time of Robertet's

---

[1] *Musée Condé*, Chantilly.

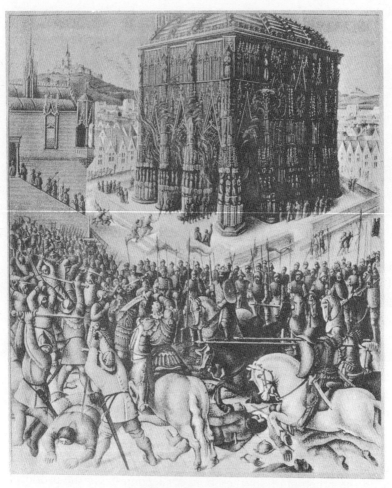

PLATE XLV (*see page* 117)
THE DESTRUCTION OF THE TEMPLE
Antiquités Judaïques
Paris: Bibliothèque Nationale (MS. fr. 247)
[*to face page* 111]

writing, the book was not complete and that nine was the correct number of miniatures which it then contained. But, if the two remaining pages were added, they must have been added by the same artist as the preceding nine (IV-XII) since all the *ystoires*, after the first three, reveal a complete unity and a perfect relation one with another. Another suggestion, which is also within the bounds of reason, is that François Robertet made a mistake and that he counted twelve instead of fourteen, and by subtracting three for those of the 'enlumineur du Duc de Berry' he carelessly allotted the remaining nine to Jehan Foucquet. Yet a third hypothesis, however, presents itself: perhaps, indeed, Robertet's negligence was not entirely his own, and that he was influenced by someone else's error. In all the books from the library of Jacques d'Armagnac, the number of illuminated pages (*ystoires*) was inscribed at the end and there is no reason to suppose (although the inscription has since disappeared) that our Josephus was an exception to this rule. These inscriptions, moreover—especially in the books from the library of Armagnac—were often erroneous and in the second volume of the *Antiquités Judaïques* we find an illustration to this fact. Here the inscription says that the manuscript contains XIII decorated pages, but it is evident that the final cypher in the Roman figures had been added and that XII was the number originally stated. Robertet's numerical discrepancies, however, are a puzzling curiosity, on the significance of which it is tantalizing to dwell, but the interest of their inaccuracy is completely counterbalanced by the extraordinary value of his authentication of the miniatures to Jehan Foucquet of Tours.

The first impression gained from a study of the eleven final miniatures is that they are the work of a master painter who, although essentially French and possessing a knowledge of the Touraine and the pasture lands of the Loire, had been to Italy and had consciously absorbed a direct Italian influence. Such a painter, indeed, was Jehan Foucquet. He was great as a craftsman; entirely French in character and outlook and yet, by reason of his travels and wide experience, was submitted to the spell of the Italian Renaissance.

The attribution, then, by Robertet of these miniatures to Foucquet brings us no surprise and their qualities entirely conform with the pattern which we have hitherto conceived of the artist's work.

On one point Robertet leaves us uninformed: he gives no indication of the date at which the pages were painted. Most recent scholars have assigned the miniatures to a late period in the artist's life and Comte Durrieu compares them with another manuscript, the *Fleur des Histoires*[1] from the library of Armagnac, which was finished sometime before 1477. It is, moreover, almost certain that Foucquet painted all the miniatures under the special guidance of the Duc d'Armagnac and this again would fix their date to a period before 1476-7, the years of the Duc's imprisonment and death. This supposition, though vague, is the nearest point to which we can go in the dating of the miniatures.

As one turns the pages of the *Josephus* and quickly scans the painted pages of Jehan Foucquet, certain signal characteristics immediately impress themselves upon the mind and a definite conception of the artist's mood and method is quickly crystallized.

It can at once be seen that our artist is a supreme master of composition; his masses are ordered without confusion and he groups his crowds with all the skill and subtlety of an experienced theatrical producer. He reveals, moreover, a particular penchant for scenes of fighting, and as a painter of military scenes he can rival Piero della Francesca and certainly outwit Uccello, whose nursery battles and rocking-horse cavalry seem but child's play when compared with Foucquet's exciting scenes of warfare and engagement.

As a psychologist, Foucquet is no less remarkable and, even in the crowds, every individual face is important and each person is stamped with his peculiar characteristics. In landscape painting and in architectural knowledge he is incomparable, and none can equal his panoramas over the valley of the Loire, nor surpass his unaffected representations of elaborate Italianate buildings standing side by side with Gothic churches and small French village

[1] MSS. fr. 55-58 (Bibliothèque Nationale).

PLATE XLVI (*see page* 118)
THE CLEMENCY OF CYRUS
Antiquités Judaïques
Paris: Bibliothèque Nationale (MS. fr. 247)
[*to face page* 113]

streets, with timbered houses and slated roofs. As a craftsman, Foucquet was a complete master. Not even Van Eyck could have found fault with his knowledge of perspective and his sense of space composition; in all the matters of artistic science, he was instinctively proficient and the problems which were to baffle the Italians for yet another century left him undismayed. It is, however, in his ravishing colour scheme that Foucquet is most miraculous and his reds and blues and brimstone yellows burn themselves upon the mind like some entrancing fire. It could, in fact, almost be said that Foucquet with his mastery of composition, his sense of landscape painting, and his profound expression of life, was a complete artist and, indeed, it would be a discontented person who could possibly desire more. But even great masters of art have their limitations and Foucquet was no exception. As a painter of life and nature he was supreme, but when his subject demanded something beyond the bounds of these two cardinal points, Foucquet found himself at a loss. His conception is material and realism is the keynote of his art. The wings of fantasy never bore away our artist of Tours and it is by the canons of practice and experience, rather than those of suggestion and imagination, that he must be judged.

The first miniature in the *Josephus* which we know to be by Foucquet, and the fourth in the volume, represents the 'Combat of the Hebrews against the Canaanites' and the 'Punishment of Korah, Dathan, and Abiron' (Plate XXXIX). This miniature has one special quality common to the first illuminated page in the book, which does not occur again in the entire manuscript: it possesses, at the top, a little tympanum in which God the Father is seen in Glory. The existence of this tympanum has aroused much discussion, since it is an unexpected element in a miniature dating from the period of 1477 and recalls an earlier epoch; it is, indeed, the echo of an old-fashioned style such as was popular in the early part of the century and particularly at the time of the Duc de Berry. The reason here for Foucquet's use of the tympanum would be difficult to explain unless it were likely that he was filling in an outline traced by his predecessor, the ducal illuminator, and thus conforming to a past pattern. The entire page, indeed, has an old-fashioned tang and does not reveal the compositional unity which we associate with our artist. It may be, therefore, that Foucquet did less than fill in a framework and merely painted in a complete design outlined by the mysterious *enlumineur*.

Like the three preceding miniatures, this *ystoire* is arranged in episodic order, although the scheme is here far less complicated and the episodes are reduced to two. In the foreground is a furious *mêlée* of soldiers, Canaanites and Hebrews (*Foucquet, le peintre militaire!*) in which horses and camels join in combat, whilst above the rocks, which form a kind of stratified wall to the battlefield (a trick which Foucquet frequently employed), is a grassy plain where the second episode reveals itself. Here we see the revolt against Moses and the divine punishment of the three princes of the Synagogue. On the left, we look into the interior of the Jewish place of worship (an Italian hall, with Corinthian columns and a Gothic altar frontal!) which is filled with priests and Levites, whilst on the right, a group of Hebrews show their terror at the spectacle of Korah, Dathan and Abiron being swallowed up into the earth and of other rebels being consumed by a sheet of flame from Heaven. During the course of these catastrophes, Moses remains apart in prayer upon a hillock.

The next miniature, the 'Siege of Jericho' (Plate XL), is the first of the more modern series where the ancient method of episodic representation is completely discarded and the incidents are welded into a perfect unity of subject.

In the foreground of this miniature, Joshua, in a gilded tunic over a blue robe and wearing a golden peaked cap, directs his orders by means of a baton; before him files a great procession in which seven persons sound the famous trumpets, and the Ark of the Covenant is being borne by four Levites in white albs with gold apparels. Seven torches are raised above the Ark and behind them a censer is being swung.

PLATE XLVII (*see page* 119)
ENTRY OF PTOLEMY INTO JERUSALEM
Antiquités Judaïques
Paris: Bibliothèque Nationale (MS. fr. 247)
[*to face page* 114]

In the background, we see the city of Jericho, with fallen walls and burning houses from which the inhabitants are rushing to meet the Jews' attacks. The miniature reveals a bizarre mixture of conception and styles. Into the figures in the foreground Foucquet has attempted to instil a certain local colour; their faces are Eastern and their costumes are also definitely Oriental. But in the background there is no trace of any such exoticism; Jericho is a homely French town—perhaps the city of Tours—with gabled houses, narrow streets and timbered façades, whilst the Jordan valley is an undisguised representation of the emerald landscape of the Loire. In this beautiful page, Foucquet's mastery of composition and perspective is at once in evidence: the crowd of persons which form the procession is kept completely under control and the landscape background is a miracle of naturalism and perfect draughtsmanship.

The succeeding miniature, the 'Downfall of the Sons of Eli' (Plate XLI), reveals another battle scene in which we see the final stages of a deadly combat. One side seems to be on the verge of defeat and the leader lies motionless in the foreground. Another captain of the same side continues fighting, brandishing a double-edged sword. This incident of slaughter and mutilation is taking place at the base of a steep rock of cylindrical shape, which runs down to the bank of the river. In the background, embedded in a deep valley, is the fortified city of Ashdod, into which the conquering Philistines, with the Ark of the Covenant, are making their entry. Here again, the artist's sense of exotic local colour deserts him and Ashdod is entirely French in appearance with the exception of a circular domed building rising in its midst, which suggests an echo of Foucquet's Italian experience.

The following decorated page, which heralds Josephus's seventh book, represents 'The Lament of David over the Death of Saul' (Plate XLII). David, in extremes of grief, tears his clothing as he hears the tidings brought by the young Amalekite, who, kneeling,

presents to David the crown and golden shoulder-plates of the
dead king.

The setting of this tragic scene is a lovely landscape in which a
river, flowing through a rocky valley, directs its course towards
a range of snow-capped mountains. On the right bank, in the
distance, can be seen the flames of a burning town. In this miniature the valley seems too harsh and rocky to suggest the verdant
plains of the Loire and immediately recalls the region of the Meuse
such as we see it in the paintings of the Fleming, Patinir.

The eighth frontispiece, and the fifth by Jehan Foucquet, is, perhaps, the most important of the series and represents 'The
Building of the Temple at Jerusalem' (Plate XLIII). The process
of construction is being performed under the eyes of Solomon,
who directs activities from a small loggia placed at the corner of
a palace which faces the Temple. On the palace, a weather-vane
bears the three lily-flowers, the emblem of the French Royal
House.

This miniature is a treasury of interest and a spring-board for
provocative speculation; here Foucquet's accurate perception
of the activities of everyday life can at once be seen. On the roof
of the Temple, a great wheel is erected to act as a crane for hoisting
up the materials of building. Below, in the foreground, workmen
are employed in all manner of labours: hewing stones, carving
statues, emptying a cask for a mould, forging an iron crow-bar,
preparing mortar or carrying water in buckets.

The Temple, which they are so busily engaged in building,
stands in a courtyard on a pavement of blazing brimstone-yellow.
It is a cubic edifice of which the fabric is stone, but, up to about
three-quarters of the height, the fabric and all the ornamentation
are covered with a layer of gold.

Here, in the architectural element, we see again Jehan Foucquet's
delicious mixture of styles, both native and foreign. The Temple,
with its three great Gothic porches and its rich ornamentation of
innumerable statues, is, in style, entirely French of the second

half of the fifteenth century, whereas the palace which adjoins it, with its violet tiles, elegant pilasters, and Corinthian columns of blue marble, suggests the architectural modes of lands beyond the Alps. This building, however, is not entirely Italian, since it can boast of a spire, a weather-vane and a sumptuous window decoration which are as Gothic as is the uncompleted Temple.

The technical achievement which this miniature reveals is little short of miraculous, and it reflects the two cardinal characteristics which make its artist fit to rank amongst the greatest in the history of painting: a mastery of design and draughtsmanship and a complete understanding of the varied aspects of human life.

The ninth miniature, depicting 'Salmanazar leading into captivity the Ten Tribes of Egypt' (Plate XLIV), reveals a more definite research after local colour. The King of Assyria sits in a chariot drawn by white horses and draped in purple hangings, whilst on the chariot are a pennon and banner displaying some imaginary armorial device suggesting pagan royal lineage. Behind the chariot, are two Oriental personages on camels, whilst near them, menaced by a stick brandished by yet another Oriental who leans from a window of the chariot, are the ten prisoners, with their hands tied behind their backs and their bodies roped together by a cord of which the end is held by the King in his right hand. The setting, however, is far from being Oriental and again it is the Touraine.

The next frontispiece, preceding Part X of Josephus's work, represents the 'Taking of Jerusalem by Nebuzar-Adan, General of the Host of Nebuchadnezzar, and the Destruction of the Temple' (Plate XLV), an episode which marked the turning point in the decline of the kingdom of Judaea. In the foreground we see one of Foucquet's favourite *mêlées* in which soldiers, in fifteenth-century costume, attack and massacre the city's inhabitants. In the background are the palace and the Temple, exactly as they were in the picture of the construction, except that the Temple is now fully built, with its entire façade covered in gold and with a vaulted roof of Italianate design,[1] and that the shallow wall enclosing the Temple court, which we saw the workmen making in the last miniature, is now completed. The palace and the courtyard are the same as before and again we are struck by the contrast of colours, especially the violet of the palace façade and the brimstone of the Temple pavement.

This time the scene is one of great agitation; soldiers are invading the palace whilst others rush to set fire to the Temple with lighted torches. In the distance we can see the city of Jerusalem, which again is Tours, or some French town, shamelessly undisguised. On the horizon are hills with a distant town and castle.

The eleventh frontispiece, the 'Clemency of Cyrus' (Plate XLVI), is one of the masterpieces of the volume. It represents the Persian King in a mood of clemency permitting the Hebrews to return to their country and to rebuild the Temple of Jerusalem. Cyrus, crown on head, clothed in a violet robe shot with gold, sits on a low throne which is draped with a cloth of white and gold. The canopy above the throne has an embroidered edge of animal designs. On either side of the King are dignitaries of his court, whilst before him kneel the Jews in expectation of the royal decision.

The setting of this miniature is particularly interesting and reveals an Italian influence more uniform than that of any of its predecessors. Cyrus sits in a paved court under a marble portico, supported by marble columns with gilded Corinthian capitals and golden rings at half their height. The wall at the back which encloses the court is surmounted by a Roman triumphal arch, decorated with finely chiselled sculptures in classical style. Before the arch stands a solitary marble Corinthian column which acts as a pedestal for a gilded figure of a man in armour. Beyond the wall, is another verdant landscape with a little house half hidden

[1] Cp. Pantheon in Rome.

PLATE XLVIII (*see page* 120)
POMPEY IN THE TEMPLE OF JERUSALEM
Antiquités Judaïques
Paris: Bibliothèque Nationale (MS. fr. 247)
[*to face page* 119]

in the trees and a castle on a hill. Here, once again, Imperial Rome with its courts and palaces is forgotten, and the castle and the homely gabled house come straight from the banks of the Loire.

The next miniature, 'The Entry of Ptolemy into Jerusalem' (Plate XLVII), is hardly less interesting than its predecessor. Before a building of which the window is ornamented with a Gothic framework and out of which several people are looking, Ptolemy advances on a white charger; he wears golden armour, a blue cloak, and a helmet surmounted by the royal crown. The pose of Ptolemy, with his baton resting on his right thigh and the drapery on the back of the horse, recalls certain figures of *condottieri* in both Italian paintings and sculpture of the fifteenth century. One is, indeed, irresistibly reminded of Donatello's Colleoni Statue. The scene is set in an open space leading to the main street of the city; on the right, the Jews are being massacred whilst all through the city the streets are lined with people awaiting the entry of the Macedonian King. Jerusalem's highway is entirely French, with little Gothic gables and spick-and-span red roofs, but in the distance is the Temple once again transformed and, since its destruction, rebuilt and refurbished at Cyrus's command with two small towers, each supporting a golden dome. Opposite the Temple can be seen the roof of the palace with its weather-vane and spire.

The thirteenth frontispiece, and the penultimate of Volume I, representing the 'Combat of Jonathas and Simon Macchabeus against Bacchides, the general of Demetrius's army', brings us back once more to the banks of the Jordan. The incident chosen by the artist is the moment when Jonathas and his companions decide to flout the enemy host by swimming the river. Among the general *mêlée* of soldiers are several mounted on horses, of which the enormous girth is not the result of the artist's exaggeration but a proof of his veracity, since this type of horse was much in use in battle at the time at which Foucquet painted.

The scene, again, is typically French and the banks of the Jordan are still the emerald pastures of the river Loire.

The next miniature, representing 'Pompey in the Temple of Jerusalem' (Plate XLVIII), brings us to the close of the first volume of Josephus's treatise and heralds the fourteenth section of the text. Here we see Pompey, fresh from the victory of the capture of Jerusalem, entering the Temple but respecting the sacred edifice. In the background is the Triumvir, standing between the altar and the coffer containing the Temple's treasure, which a priest is resignedly showing him; in the middle distance are the Roman soldiers standing in orderly attention. In the immediate foreground, the massacre of the Jews is still in progress; many are dead or dying and one aged man implores the mercy of a Roman soldier.

Like many of its predecessors, this miniature contains a striking architectural element and here there is even more to interest us than before. Again we see a bizarre blend of architectural styles. The altar, covered with a red cloth and furnished with seven finely carved candlesticks, is such as might have been seen in any church in France; on either side of the altar are pedestals supporting angels holding torches, all in golden metal; these pedestals are connected by rods which support green curtains. The disposition of the altar and its appurtenances is entirely orthodox and conforms to a fashion common in French churches both at that time and in the present day. Immediately above the altar the artist has ingeniously placed the Ark of the Covenant, supported, on either side, by two large cherubim both chased in gold and standing on columns of blue marble.[1]

Our eye is now attracted by certain other elements which strike an unusual note and recall the influence of Italy; the choir, for

[1] This representation may be aptly compared with the first miniature of the Annunciation in the Hours of Chantilly, where the Virgin receives the Angel in the Chapel Royal of Bourges or Paris (cp. Pl. XIX). This arrangement of the Ark of the Covenant above the altar is not peculiar to Foucquet but is that of a mediaeval reliquary.

PLATE XLIX (see page 123)
ENTRANCE OF HEROD INTO JERUSALEM
Antiquités Judaïques (Vol. II)
Paris: Bibliothèque Nationale (n.a. fr. 21013)
[*to face page* 120]

instance, is separated from the main body of the building by a balustrade of green and pink porphyry symmetrically planned in lozenged-shaped designs. Such balustrades are to be seen to-day all over Italy and particularly in Rome. The entire interior of the Temple, moreover, is supported by a series of twisted columns of a very curious design. These columns are of the utmost interest and importance since Foucquet copied them from real examples, seen in Rome, of the famous *Columnae Vitineae* of St. Peter's.[1] The columns no longer exist since they vanished with the destruction of the ancient Basilica of St. Peter's in favour of the new edifice by Bramante and Michel Angelo, but we know that they were grouped to constitute a porch placed before the Confessio of St. Peter, and it seems likely that their appearance was very similar to that in our illuminated page. In the modern Basilica of St. Peter's replicas of the columns occur many times, especially in the great bronze tabernacle designed by Bernini for the high altar. A very similar design was to be seen in the fifteenth century and still exists to-day in the second great Papal Basilica in Rome, San Giovanni in Laterano.

The appearance of these famous twisted columns in the decoration of Josephus's first volume is not mere caprice, since it relates to the Roman tradition that the columns were brought to St. Peter's from Solomon's Temple at Jerusalem. Their introduction, therefore, by Foucquet into this miniature of the *Antiquités Judaïques* is but another testimony to his apt agility of mind and proportioned sense of learning.

(d) The artist of the second volume

In passing from the first to the second volume of the *Antiquités Judaïques*, a certain disappointment is inevitable. Not only is the latter volume incomplete, but it is in no way as sumptuous as its predecessor, nor, with one exception, are its decorations

---

[1] So called *Vitineae* from their pattern of vine leaves (*vitis*), amid which little winged or naked figures play.

the work of Jehan Foucquet of Tours. There is no doubt, indeed, that the second volume is the companion to the first nor that it was written at the same period, but in it much of the old glory has vanished and the fanfare of Foucquet's past splendour finds no echo. In the first volume, the calligrapher left a space at the head of each new book for the inclusion of a large, full-page miniature, but in the second only one such space was left, at the very beginning of the book as a frontispiece to Part XV. For the four remaining sections of the *Antiquités* and the seven books of the *Guerre des Juifs* the calligrapher has reserved merely a space of about $2\frac{1}{2}$ inches square, set in the middle of a column and capable of taking only a tiny miniature. This system of placing small square decorations among a double-columned text was an antiquated one and was common among book illuminators at the time of the Duc de Berry. The second volume of Josephus[1] which the Duc possessed is illustrated in this way.

The reasons for the sudden decline in splendour after the end of the fifteenth book are not definitely known, but it is likely that economy was the cause. The entire appointments of the first volume were so extraordinarily luxurious, from the binding down to the index, that the owners may well have thought fit in the second volume to rest upon their laurels. It is, indeed, by no means rare to find the miniatures at the beginning of mediaeval books more magnificent than those at the end.

The second volume, in its present condition of incompleteness, consists of ten leaves, of which two are still missing.[2] Both these missing leaves must have been adorned with small miniatures, set into the text.

The first miniature which meets our eyes upon opening the second volume does much to reassure us, since it is a full-page decoration by Foucquet himself and a continuation of the series from the preceding volume. It represents the 'Entry of Herod into

[1] Bibliothèque Nationale. Nouvelles Acquisitions, 21013.

[2] The missing leaves occur at the beginning of the prologue and before the sixth book of the *Guerre des Juifs*.

Jerusalem' (Plate XLIX) and at once we recognize certain familiar characteristics. In the centre of the picture, Herod, crowned and in golden armour, proudly advances on a white horse, of which the head and body are also protected by armour. On either side there is a scene of slaughter in which the followers of Herod massacre the Jews, many of whom are praying for mercy. On the right, the two mounted trumpeters of the invading army sound the clarion of victory. In the background we see the Temple Sanctuary and other buildings of Jerusalem, some of which have golden domes in truly Oriental fashion. The arrangement of the Sanctuary is specially interesting; before it is the 'Bath of Purification' being duly used by various persons who seem oblivious of the fact that a massacre is occurring in the Temple courts, and behind is the high altar, ornamented in French style by three Gothic niches. The bath and the chancel are separated by another Italianate balustrade and the upper section is covered by a canopy supported, as in the preceding miniature, by the *Columnae Vitineae*. At the foot of the altar, a priest swings a censer; whilst behind him, two Jews kneel in prayer.

Unfortunately, this miniature is in bad condition, the pigments being irremediably tarnished, and many of the details are indistinct. But there is no doubt that the work is that of Jehan Foucquet, since the affinities which this page bears with the last eleven miniatures of the preceding volume are innumerable. The trumpeters, for instance, recall those in the frontispiece of 'Salmanazar'; the kneeling Jews are a deliberate echo of the figures in the 'Clemency of Cyrus', and the *Columnae Vitineae* are an exact replica of those in the final decorated page of Volume I.

This full-page miniature of Herod's triumph sets the seal upon Foucquet's work in connection with Josephus, and from here onward we do not see his hand again. The ten small miniatures, which follow, seem to be the work of one artist of considerable ability and surprising qualities of style, with a definite similarity to Foucquet himself, but without the master's entrancing skill and all-embracing talent. The spell of wonderment is broken and such prodigious magnificence as was seen in the 'Clemency of Cyrus' or the 'Building of the Temple' never occurs again.

In the small miniatures much is altered; the facial type is different and the broad faces, associated with the *Tourangeaux*, give place to a more pointed, elongated type. The details, too, are changed and that delightful blend of homely incidents and startling attempts at local colour has completely vanished. Exoticism no longer exists and the settings and costumes are almost entirely French or Italian and betray no research after Oriental effects. The drawing, too, is less audacious and its correctness is due to a timid precision rather than to a progressive skill; the landscapes, moreover, though portrayed in admirable perspective, have lost their tender charm and seem no more to be enveloped in sheets of liquid sunlight.

The first small miniature of volume two represents Herod with his two sons, Alexander and Aristobulos, on their knees before the Roman Emperor. Augustus, the Emperor, is portrayed in the traditional manner of Charlemagne with a flowing beard and a long blue robe. Herod salutes the Emperor with his crown.

The scene is set in a kind of palace loggia, with a green tessellated floor and elegant pilasters; through the window can be seen a view of the sea with two ships. In accordance with the manner of mediaeval illuminators, various inscriptions are inserted on the appointments of the room, such as on the edge of the daïs and the hem of the carpet, but none is satisfactorily legible.

The second miniature, representing the arrest by Herod of his two sons, has no particular interest, but the third, that of 'Augustus nominating Quirinius as Governor of Syria', has an importance in that it reveals a certain defect of draughtsmanship of which Foucquet would have been incapable. Quirinius, having dismounted from his horse, kneels before the Emperor, but the horse is drawn by the artist as considerably smaller than his master. Such an inaccuracy at once betrays the absence of Foucquet's master hand.

The fourth miniature, the 'Assassination of Caligula', represents the Emperor's demise in the presence of a great crowd, but the scene, which under Foucquet's guidance would have been exciting and dramatic, is merely conventionalized and commonplace.

After this miniature there is a *lacuna*, which is due not to the fault of time but to the negligence of the scribe who, by some unknown circumstance, omitted to leave a space for the painter to fill with a miniature. The twentieth and final book of the *Antiquités* is left, therefore, unheralded by any painted decoration.

Another such lack occurs before the prologue of the second part of Josephus's treatise but, here, the blame can be imputed to no careless scribe but to the havoc which the passage of time has wrought upon the manuscript.

The first miniature which we possess, illustrating the *Guerre des Juifs*, represents the 'Entry into Jerusalem of Antiochus Epiphanos'. Here the artist has obviously studied Foucquet's miniatures in the preceding volume, since he has represented the Temple in the same cubic shape as before, but he has made it less Gothic and less elaborately ornamented. Only the lower part, moreover, is visible.

The next miniature illustrates an incident in the second volume of the *Guerre des Juifs* and represents 'Herod's Funeral'. Although, as a work of art, it does not far transcend the bounds of mere competence, it is invaluable as a rare historical record and reflects a custom peculiarly French. At the celebration of the obsequies of the King of France, it was customary to make an effigy in natural size of the late sovereign, and clothe it with all the attributes of royalty. The face of the effigy consisted of a death-mask taken from the actual corpse, and the taking of the mask was an honour given to the most distinguished artists of the day. During the obsequies, the officers of the court wore long mourning cloaks with hoods covering their faces. These *pleurants* were frequently represented in fifteenth century sculpture and such famous examples as the 'Tomb of the Duc de Bourgogne' at

Dijon and the 'Tomb of Philippe Pot' in the Louvre immediately spring to the mind.

In the miniature of 'Herod's Funeral' all thoughts of Jerusalem are rejected and these customs —intrinsically French—are most interestingly revealed. The royal effigy, dressed in a violet robe, lies upon a bed draped in gold and four *pleurants*, with their faces covered, kneel by its side. Guards stand on either hand, with their swords reversed as a sign of respect for the dead. The face of the effigy is clean-shaven, and here we are confronted with a vivid and illuminating detail. In the preceding miniatures Herod is represented with a flowing beard, but in the scene of the royal obsequies the artist has conformed to the French custom and has painted the King's face shaved as a preparation for his lying-in-state.

Of the four remaining miniatures[1], only the last two are of importance. The penultimate miniature of the series, 'The Massacres at Jerusalem and Dissensions among the Jews', has an interesting architectural setting. The Temple, very similar to Foucquet's conception only less Gothic and more Italianate, is in the background and in front of it are little gabled houses such as might be seen in any small French town. On the right we see part of a house which in style is purely classical Italian, with two fluted pilasters bordering an inlaid rectangular plaque. All this is an illuminating testimony that the artist of this miniature shared with Foucquet experience gained in Italy.

The last miniature of all, the 'Assault and Taking of Jerusalem by Titus', is a scene of desperate engagement such as Foucquet would have delighted in. The earth is strewn with corpses—all portrayed in excellent perspective—and at the Temple gates ensues a scene of violent fighting. Here, for the first time, we have an uninterrupted view of the Temple as the artist of the

[1]They represent: 'Vespasian marching against the Jews'; the 'Taking of the Town Gamala by the Romans' (Gamala is represented as a small French town with gabled houses and timbered façades); 'Massacres at Jerusalem'; *lacuna*, page missing; 'Assault on Temple and the Taking by Titus of Jerusalem'.

second volume conceived it. At first sight, it seems very similar to the representations of the first volume and it is apparent that the artist has studied Foucquet's rendering: the shape is still cubic and the edifice is surmounted by a low vaulted roof. But the difference lies in significant details which a second glance will reveal. In the large miniatures of the first volume the architecture of the Temple is completely French, with its galleries, porches and pinnacles and its congeries of statuary. But in the small miniatures of the companion volume, the Gothic spirit has gone and its place is taken by an insistence upon cornices, pilasters and classic forms—all the devices, in fact, which are redolent not of fifteenth century France but of the Italian *Quattrocento*.

The problem which now immediately presents itself is the identity of the artist of the ten small miniatures of the second volume, since it is already a point of general decision that their painter, although imbued with a similar doctrine, was not Jehan Foucquet himself but a different artist. Here again, Comte Durrieu's powers of deduction come into play and it is to this great scholar that we owe the most ingenious and illuminating theory of explanation. Comte Durrieu launches his argument from the secure starting point of given data. The precise date of the miniatures is unknown but their period is certain and, without question, they were executed for the Duc Jacques d'Armagnac. The clue to this affirmation is to be found in another manuscript from the Bibliothèque Nationale, the *Lancelot du Lac*,[1] which is known, by the constant repetition in the margins of the Duc's armorial device (sirens and wild men), to have been commissioned by Jacques d'Armagnac and which, by reason of an exact similarity of technique and conception, was doubtlessly decorated by the same hand as that of the ten small miniatures of the second volume. The artist, therefore, was working in the service of the Duc and would most likely have been in close contact with Jehan Foucquet. It is evident, moreover, that Jehan Foucquet employed pupils and

[1]MS. fr. 113.

it is thought that he was an influential 'maître d'atelier'. If this were so, Foucquet would most probably have followed the unwritten law of all illustrators of books that the master was responsible for the large miniatures and the pupil for the small. It is, then, most likely that the small miniatures of Volume II were painted, under Foucquet's direction, by a member of his *atelier* or by a colleague who was directly infused with his ideas.

Of the various miniaturists who are thought to have come under the influence of Jehan Foucquet and to have worked as members of his studio there are a few whose names immediately suggest themselves in this connection. One may, indeed, immediately think of Jehan de Bourdichon, the artist of the 'Grandes Heures de la Reine Anne de Bretagne'; Jehan Colombe de Bruges, an artist who enjoyed the special favour of Louis XI; and the celebrated Jehan de Montluçon. But none of these is identical with the artist of our ten small miniatures and all possess a style either superior or inferior and always completely different from anything we find in the Josephus. One may, moreover, momentarily entertain the idea of the collaboration of that prolific master who flourished at the time, the 'excellent peintre François', thus called by Robert Gaguin in a letter. But there again the trail is false and the excellent François is not the artist with whom we are concerned.

It remains, therefore, for us to search for our solution among works which obviously belong to the same school but which were executed by unidentified artists. In this category, the two books which Comte Durrieu quotes as being most nearly related to our miniatures are the *Tite Live de la Sorbonne* and the *Tite Live de Versailles*, both in the Bibliothèque Nationale.[1] Of these, the latter immediately concerns our argument.

The *Tite Live de Versailles* contains a frontispiece and a series of small miniatures which, although bearing a close resemblance to Foucquet's own work, reveal a slightly less skilled touch than that of the master's hand which brings them into a direct line with the ten small miniatures of Volume II. In every way are they

[1] MSS. fr. 20071, 20072.

PLATE L (see page 133)
A ROMAN LEGATE
Drawing
London: Collection of Henry Oppenheimer, Esq.
[to face page 129]

related: in technique and mannerisms; in architectural formulae; in colour scheme and composition. It is, then, with much reason that Durrieu attributed these problematic paintings to the 'master of the *Tite Live de Versailles*'.

Up to this point, Durrieu's theory, though excellent and sound, does not particularize and it is with great audacity and ingenuity that he goes further to produce a name. It need hardly be said that in this second section of his argument, Durrieu was making no declaration of authentication but only proffering a seductive theory of which the truth will probably never be known. His sphere, therefore, is pure hypothesis and was never intended to be accepted as established fact.

Durrieu recalls that it was at one time considered that the miniatures of the second volume were the work of one of Foucquet's two sons, either Louis or François. Of Louis we know nothing and around François complete silence reigns unless it is to him that the 'excellent peintre' mentioned by Gaguin refers. Were this the case, the small miniatures are certainly not his work, for the style of the 'peintre François' is entirely different from that of the Josephus pages. But Brèche, the lawyer and the contemporary authority to whom we owe the knowledge that Foucquet had any sons, mentions in the same reference an artist, Jehan Poyet, whom he considers as superior in technique of painting to any of the Foucquets, either sons or father.[1]

Now, although it is entirely unlikely that Jehan Poyet excelled the elder Foucquet, he must, notwithstanding, have been a considerable artist. His praise is sung by Jean Lemaire de Belges and Jean Pèlerin le Viateur, both of which excellent critics and proportionate arbiters of taste place him immediately after Foucquet and even suggest that there was some connection between the two painters. We know, moreover, that Poyet executed '23 ystoires riches' in the famous *Petites Heures d'Anne de Bourgogne*, but these, alas, have vanished.

It is not, therefore, impossible that Poyet was the artist of the

[1]Cp. p. 34.

small miniatures in the second volume of our Josephus; from his frequent mention in connection with Foucquet it seems that Poyet may well have been infused with Foucquet's ideas and, perhaps, even, he had been his pupil. He was certainly younger than Jehan Foucquet, since he painted the Hours for Anne of Burgundy in 1495-6, fifteen years after Foucquet's death. The small miniatures, moreover, reveal just that sense of youth and surprising mastery of technique which Brèche and others praise. This correlation, therefore, between Josephus and Jean Poyet is an ingenious assumption which, although not certain, is not improbable, and it only remains for the discovery of Anne of Burgundy's *Book of Hours* finally to reassure us.

Such, then, is the entangled story of Foucquet's connection with Josephus, and the few points of evidence which pierce the mystery are as welcome as solitary stars on a murky London night. Throughout the whole confused history of the life and work of Jehan Foucquet we are constantly tantalized by a lack of evidence just at the moment when information is most required, or are baffled by a textual *lacuna* for which only negligence or vandalism has been responsible. There is, however, one figure to whom all gratitude is due and that is the librarian Robertet, without whose note in the Josephus no single work of Tour's great native would have been authenticated. To him we owe the knowledge which is the foundation stone of all our criticism and the starting-point of all our hypotheses. Without Robertet, an even denser veil of mystery would enshroud the figure of Jehan Foucquet and still less would have been known about this sensitive connoisseur of life and consummate landscape painter who, from his dim studio tucked away between two towers in the narrow streets of Tours, flung a window wide open on to Nature and disclosed an entrancing, joyous panorama of the ever-green Touraine.

PART FOUR

APPENDICES

APPENDIX I

DRAWINGS ATTRIBUTED TO JEHAN FOUCQUET

THE CELEBRATED and beautiful drawing of the 'Roman Legate' (Plate L), in the possession of Mr. Henry Oppenheimer, can be considered to be the master's work. It has an extraordinary vitality and reflects that refined simplicity and acute sense of life which we associate with the later work of Foucquet, upon which the influence of Italy had made its mark. The drawing is made in silver point on ivory paper and in the top right-hand corner runs the inscription: 'Ung Romain légat de n . . . St. père en France'.

In the Berlin Kupferstichkabinett there is a drawing—probably a portrait of Jouvenel des Ursins (Plate LI)—which has, with reason, been attributed to Jehan Foucquet and which is irresistibly reminiscent of the portrait of the Chancellor in the Louvre (cp. Plate IV). The drawing was originally in the Sammlung Rumohr, where it was catalogued under Holbein, but Dr. Friedländer in an article in the *Jahrbuch*[1] was the first to notice its resemblance to Foucquet's work and to consider it as a study for the Louvre portrait. This drawing reveals an impressive vivacity and learned realism which recall the praise of Foucquet's contemporaries of his skill in portraiture and the dictum of his friend Filarète that none better than Foucquet could make a portrait instinct with the breath of life. The drawing is made in charcoal and coloured chalks upon a grey-toned paper, and is the earliest known example of this rare combination of media.

Monsieur Pierre Lavallée in a recent book upon French drawings[2] mentions two other works which come into line with our artist of Tours; of these the more likely to be by Foucquet is the 'Portrait of a Man'—drawn in charcoal and sanguine—in the Hermitage Museum of Leningrad. Like the preceding drawing,

[1]XXXI (1910), page 227.   [2]Cp. Bibliography, page 141.

this work was also attributed to Holbein and it remained for Monsieur Guiffrey in an article in *Les Arts*[1] to give it to an unknown French artist of the fifteenth century and to compare it, by reason of its individuality and beautiful precision and its lack of any trace of coarseness or exaggeration, to the work of Jehan Foucquet or of some distinguished colleague or contemporary.

The second drawing mentioned in this connection is the 'Portrait of a Man' formerly in the Liechtenstein Collection and now in the Albertina at Vienna. The man is standing full-face, with his right hand resting on a cane. On the left are two little dogs. This drawing was first attributed to Foucquet by Dr. Meder, who saw in it both a refinement of characterization and a skill in the arrangement of the draperies which were reminiscent of the technical excellence of our great painter.

[1]Sept. 1906.

APPENDIX II

THE 'AIR DE PARENTÉ' BETWEEN THE *ANTIQUITÉS JUDAÏQUES* AND THE *TRÈS RICHES HEURES DU DUC DE BERRY*

IT HAS already been seen that a resemblance exists between the first three miniatures of the Josephus manuscript and the famous *Très Riches Heures* of the Duc de Berry at Chantilly which was sufficiently strong to have persuaded certain early critics that the mysterious *enlumineur* was responsible for the two works.

Monsieur Durrieu, however, has revealed, once and for all, that the miniatures by Pol de Limbourg in the manuscript at Chantilly are masterpieces of the most supreme beauty of colour and draughtsmanship and of the highest perfection of composition, and that they leave our preliminary pages of Josephus's book far behind in every facet of the artistic canon. The theory, then, that the ducal *enlumineur* was Pol de Limbourg himself is entirely exploded.

But, even though there may be no identity, there is certainly a resemblance between the two works which cannot be denied, and a definite 'air de parenté' may be established. In the management of the planes, the treatment of the rocks, the grouping of the figures and the blending of the tones, the two sets of miniatures have many points of harmony, and in certain stylistic details the likeness is very apparent. The tympanum, for example, in the first miniature of the Josephus book, which encloses the figure of God the Father, occurs twice in the *Très Riches Heures*[1] and the rainbow in the same miniature which bears the signs of the Zodiac recalls a compositional style common to all the pages of the calendar of the manuscript at Chantilly. The animals, too, with

[1] Cp. Comte Durrieu's monograph on the *Très Riches Heures*, Pls. LV and LX.

135

which Josephus's *Earthly Paradise* abounds, recall most strongly those in certain pages of the *Très Riches Heures*.[1] Other points of contact can, moreover, be traced in the *Très Belles Heures du Duc de Berry* in the Rothschild Collection, in which two miniatures may be considered as the close companions of the finer and more luxurious *Très Riches Heures*.

Comte Durrieu's comparisons, however, do not end here, and his long and laborious researches were rewarded by his discovery of further analogies in certain other works. In a copy of *Térence* (Bib. Nat. MS. Lat. 7907, fols. 63, 83, 84, etc.), given to the Duc de Berry in 1408; in a *Roman de la Rose* (Bib. Nat. MS. fr. 380, fols. 19 38, 85), also belonging to the Duke; and in a Pontifical (Bib. Nat. MS. Lat. 8886, fols. 101, 105, 130, etc.), which the Duc presented to the Sainte Chapelle at Bourges, he found stylistic tendencies which reminded him irresistibly of the *Très Riches Heures* and of our first three painted pages in the Josephus manuscript. Affinities were also found in the Geneva Boccaccio (Bibl. de Genève, MS. fr. 190) and in a painting of the Coronation of the Virgin in a Book of Hours at the British Museum (Addit. MS. 32454, fol. 46). These resemblances, however, do not indicate that all the works are from the same hand but signify merely that they were prompted by the same artistic stimulus. In colouring, landscape painting, perspective, and arrangement of the costumes they reflect an affinity with the *Très Riches Heures* and their quality, although it does not equal the standard of Maître Pol de Limbourg himself, is sufficiently high to allow them to be labelled as works of Pol de Limbourg's school.

It is, indeed, from this point that Comte Durrieu launched his supposition that the first three miniatures of our Josephus were the work of Pol de Limbourg's brothers, Jehannequin and Hermand, who were among his most ardent collaborators and who, without attaining the master's supreme degree of excellence, would most certainly have absorbed his influence and have created works which, like our first three miniatures, were inferior but very definite reflections of their brother Pol's transcendent skill.

[1] Cp. *ibid*. Pl. LVIII.

BIBLIOGRAPHY

AVERULINO, called ANTONIO FILARÈTE. Architectural treatise published by Dr. Wolfgang von Oettingen (under the title of 'Tractat über die Baukunst') in the collection of *Quellenschriften zur Kunstgeschichte des Mittelalters und der Neuzeit*, neue Folge, III. Band. Wien, 1890.

BABELON, ERNEST. 'Les Origines de la Médaille en France', in the *Revue de l'art ancien et moderne*, t. XVII, 1905, pp. 161-179 and 277-294.

BASTARD D'ETANG, COMTE AUGUSTE DE. Various articles reprinted in the works of Curmer, Delisle, and Paulin, Paris.

BERTAUX, EMILE. 'Foucquet, Jehan.' Article in *La Grande Encyclopédie*, t. XVII, pp. 875-877.

BODE, WILHELM VON. 'Die Fürstliche Liechtenstein'sche Galerie in Wien; Die Französische Schule'; published in *Die Graphischen Künste*, 1895, p. 109.

BOUCHOT, HENRI. 'Jean Foucquet.' Articles with illustrations in the *Gazette des Beaux-Arts*, 1890, t. II, pp. 273-281 and p. 416-426.
   'L'Exposition des Primitifs Français; quelques Portraits de Jean Fouquet aujourd'hui perdus.' Article in the *Revue de l'art ancien et moderne*, t. XIII, 1903, pp. 1-22.
   Les Primitifs Français, Paris, 1904.

BRÈCHE, JEHAN. *Joannis Brechaei, Turoni Juriconsulti, ad Titulum Pandectarum de verborum et rerum significatione commentarii.* Lyon, 1556. In folio.

BURTY, PHILIPPE. 'Jean Fouquet; le Livre d'Heures de Maistre Estienne Chevalier.' Article in the *Gazette des Beaux-Arts*, 1866, t. I, pp. 394-397.

'Jean Fouquet; les Heures d'Estienne Chevalier; les Antiquités Judaïques, etc. *Ibid.*, 1868, t. I, pp. 187-193.
Catalogue des Manuscrits de Chantilly.
Catalogue de l'Exposition des Primitifs Français.

BYVANCK, A. W. *Les principaux MSS. à peintures de la Bibliothèque Royale des Pays Bas à la Haye*, 1924, pp. 81-88, Pl. XXXIX.

CHALMEL, J. L. *Tablettes chronologiques de l'histoire civile et ecclésiastique de Touraine*, Tours, 1818.
Histoire de Touraine, Tours, 1828. 4 vols.

CHAMPEAUX, A. DE, and CAUCHERY, P. *Les Travaux d'art exécutés pour Jean de France, duc de Berry*, Paris, 1894.

CHESNEAU, ERNEST. 'Jean Fouquet, Heures de Maistre Etienne Chevalier.' Article in the *Constitutionnel*, 18th March, 1866.

COLLINGWOOD, W. G. *Art Journal*, 1882, pp. 337-339.

COMMYNES, *Mémoires de Philippe de*, Pub. Garnier, Paris.

COURAJOD, LOUIS. Article relating to Foucquet's Italian Journey in the *Bulletin de la Société des Antiquaires de France*, 1887, pp. 299-300.

CRESPY-LE-PRINCE. *La Fille de Fouquet.* Novel reprinted in the *Chroniques sur les Cours de France*, Paris, 1834.

CURMER, LOUIS. *L'Œuvre de Jehan Fouquet*, Paris, 1866. 2 vols. Contains reprints of articles by de Bastard, de la Borde, Vallet de Viriville, Ferdinand Denis, etc.

DELISLE, LÉOPOLD. *Le Cabinet des Manuscrits de la Bibliothèque Nationale*, Paris, 1868-1881. 3 vols.
Les Livres d'Heures du duc de Berry, Paris, 1884. Reprinted almost in full in the *Gazette des Beaux-Arts*, 1884, t. I.
'La Cité de Dieu de Saint Augustin, illustrée d'après les indications de Robert Gaguin.' Article in the *Journal des Savants*, 1898, pp. 563-568.
Article on the gift made to France by Mr. Yates Thompson of the second volume of the Josephus in the *Comptes rendus de l'Académie des Inscriptions et Belles-Lettres*, 1905, pp. 523-525, and 1906, p. 4.
Article on the gift made to France by the King of England in the same publication, 1906, pp. 87-89, and p. 106.

BIBLIOGRAPHY

DENIS, FERDINAND. *Histoire de l'Ornementation des Manuscrits.* The chapter on Foucquet is reprinted in Curmer's *L'Œuvre de Jehan Fouquet.*

DUPLESSIS, GEORGES. Reference to a fragment of the Chantilly Hours acquired by the Bibliothèque Nationale in the *Bulletin de la Société Nationale des Antiquaires de France,* 1881, pp. 78-80.

DURRIEU, COMTE PAUL. *Une peinture historique de Jean Fouquet: le roi Louis XI tenant un chapitre de l'ordre de Saint Michel,* Paris, 1891.

Un quarante-quatrième fragment des Heures de Maître Etienne Chevalier, retrouvé au musée du Louvre, Paris (*Bulletin des Musées*), 1891.

Une vue intérieure de l'ancien Saint Pierre de Rome au milieu du quinzième siècle, peinte par Jean Foucquet, Rome, 1892.

'Deux Miniatures Inédites de Jean Foucquet'. Article in the *Mémoires de la Société Nationale des Antiquaires de France,* t. LXI.

'Un Chef d'œuvre de la miniature française sous Charles VIII.' Article in *Le Manuscrit,* février 1894.

Chantilly, Les Très Riches Heures du Duc de Berry, Paris, 1904.

'La Question des Œuvres de Jeunesse de Jehan Fouquet.' Article in the *Recueil de Mémoires,* published on the centenary of the Société des Antiquaires de France, Paris, 1904.

'Le Maître des Heures du Maréchal de Boucicaut.' Article in the *Revue de L'Art ancien et moderne,* 1906, ts. XIX and XX.

'La Légende et l'histoire de Jean Fouquet.' Article in the *Annuaire-Bulletin de la Société de l'histoire de France,* Paris, 1907.

Exposition des Primitifs Français, Paris, 1904. Contributions to the Catalogue.

Les 'Antiquités Judaïques' et le Peintre, Jean Foucquet.[1] Paris, 1910.

[1] This book, the *magnum opus* on the subject of Foucquet, contains a full and profoundly studied bibliography which, in its wide range and eclectic choice, is incomparably important for scholars and students of the subject of mediæval book illustration in France.

Le Boccace de Munich, Paris and Munich, 1910.

'La Peinture en France de 1422-1489', in the *Histoire de l'Art* of André Michel, t. IV², pp. 723-730, Paris, 1911.

Livre d'Heures peint par Jean Foucquet pour Maître Etienne Chevalier: le quarante-cinquième feuillet retrouvé en Angleterre. Pamphlet printed for the Members of the Société Française de Reproductions de Manuscrits à peintures, 1923.

FLORIO, FRANCESCO. *Francisci Florii, Florentini, ad Jacobum Tarlatum Castellionensem, de probatione Turonica.* Reprinted in Curmer's *L'Œuvre de Jehan Fouquet.*

FRIEDLÄNDER, MAX. 'Die Votivtafel des Estienne Chevalier von Fouquet.' Article in the *Jahrbuch der Kgl. Preussischen Kunstsammlungen*, Band XVII, 1896, pp. 206-214.
'Eine Bildnisstudie Jean Fouquets.' *Ibid.*, Band XXXI, 1910, p. 227.

GABROL ET LECLERCQ. 'Livres d'Heures. Article in the *Dictionnaire d'Archéologie Chrétienne et de Liturgie*, t. IX², pp. 1835 sqq.

GAUCHERY, PAUL. *Influence de Jean de France, duc de Berry, sur le développement de l'Architecture et des Arts*, Caen, 1901.

GIRAUDET, E. *Les Artistes Tourangeaux*, Tours, 1885.

GRANDMAISON, CHARLES DE. 'Document sur Jean Fouquet', in the *Revue des Sociétés Savantes*, 1866, 2e semestre, pp. 502-503.

Documents inédits pour servir à l'histoire des Arts en Touraine, Tours, 1870. (Vol. XX of the *Mémoires de la Société Archéologique de Touraine*.)

GRUYER, F. A. 'Etienne Chevalier et son patron Saint Etienne par Jean Fouquet.' Article in the *Gazette des Beaux-Arts*, 1896, t. I, pp. 89-100.
Chantilly: les Quarante Foucquet, Paris, 1897.
Chantilly: Musée Condé. Notice des Peintures, Paris, 1899.

GUIFFREY, J. *Inventaires de Jean, Duc de Berry*, Paris, 1894 and 1896. 2 vols.

'Un portrait Français du xve siècle à Pétersbourg.' Article in *Les Arts*, Paris, 1906, September.

HULIN DE LOO, GEORGES. *Inventaires de Marguerite d'Autriche*, Paris, 1839. 2 vols.

JANIN, JULES. 'Jehan Foucquet.' Article in the *Journal des Débats*, July 1865. Reprinted by Curmer in his *Œuvre de Jean Fouquet*.
'Jehan Fouquet, peintre du quinzième siècle.' Anonymous article in the *Magazin Pittoresque*, t. XXVII, 1859, pp. 372-373.

LABARTE, JULES. *Histoire des Arts industriels au moyen âge*, Paris, 1864-1865. 3 vols.

LABORDE, COMTE DE (later MARQUIS LEON DE). *Les Ducs de Bourgogne*, Paris, 1849-1852. 3 vols.
La Renaissance des Arts à la Cour de France, vol. I, Paris, 1850-1855.

LABORDE, COMTE A. DE. *La Cité de Dieu de Saint Augustin.* 3 vols. Paris, 1909.

LAFENESTRE, GEORGES. *Jehan Fouquet*, Paris, 1905.
'L'Homme au Verre de Vin attribué à Fouquet', in the *Revue de l'Art ancien et moderne*, vol. XX, 1906, pp. 437-440.

LAVALLÉE, PIERRE. *Le Dessin Français du XIIIᵉ au XVIᵉ Siècles*, Paris, 1930, pp. 18-19, 68-70.

LAVISSE, ERNEST. *Histoire de France*, t. IV¹, pp. 194-227.

LEIDINGER. *Meisterwerke der Buchmalerei*, 1920, pl. 35.

LEMAIRE DE BELGES, JEAN. *La Plaincte du Désiré.* *Les Illustrations de Gaule et Singularités de Troye.*
La Couronne Margaritique.

LEPRIEUR, PAUL. Articles in the *Revue de l'Art ancien et moderne*: 1895, t. I, p. 25; t. II, pp. 15, 147, 347. 1897, t. I, pp. 25-41; t. II, pp. 15-30, 147-160, 347-359.

MANDROT, BERNARD DE. 'Jacques d'Armagnac, duc de Nemours.' Articles in the *Revue Historique*, 1890, t. XLIII, pp. 274-316; t. XLIV, pp. 241-312.

MARQUET DE VASSELOT, J. J. 'Deux émaux de Jean Fouquet.' Article in the *Gazette des Beaux-Arts*, 1904, t. II, pp. 140-148.

MARTENS, BELLA. *Meister Francke*, Hamburg, 1929.

JEHAN FOUCQUET: NATIVE OF TOURS

MARTIN, HENRI. *Les Miniaturistes Français*, Paris, 1906.
Les Peintres de Manuscrits et la Miniature en France, Paris, 1909.
Les Fouquet de Chantilly, Paris, 1926.
Series of *Collections Publiques de France*.

MEDER, DR. (cf. Schönbrunner u. Meder). *Handzeichnungen alter Meister aus der Albertina und anderen Sammlungen*, p. 655.

MELY, FERNAND DE. 'Une Promenade aux Primitifs.' Article in the *Revue de l'Art ancien et moderne*, t. XV, 1904, pp. 453-468.
'L'Émail de Jehan Fouquet au Louvre', in the *Gazette des Beaux-Arts*, 1905, t. II, pp. 281-287.

MICHIELS, ALFRED. *Miniaturen des Jehan Fouquet im Besitze des Herrn Louis Brentano*, Frankfurt a/M., 1855.

MOLINIER, EMILE. *L'Émaillerie*, Paris, 1891.

MONTAIGLON, ANATOLE DE. *Jean Foucquet et son portrait du Pape Eugène IV* in the *Archives de l'Art Français*, 2nd series, t. I, 1861, pp. 454-468. Reprinted by Curmer in his *L'Œuvre de Jean Fouquet*.

NAGLER, G. K. *Neues Allgemeines Künstler-Lexicon*, München, 1835-1892. 22 vols.

OMONT, HENRI. 'Antiquités et Guerre des Juifs de Josèphe offertes à la Bibliothèque.' Article in the *Bibliothèque de l'Ecole de Chartes*, t. LXVII, 1906, pp. 157-159.
Antiquités et Guerre des Juifs, reproduction des 25 miniatures, Paris.
Grandes Chroniques de France, enluminées par Jehan Fouquet, Paris.

PAULIN, PARIS. *Les Grandes Chroniques de France*, Paris, 1836-1838. 6 vols.

PASSAVANT, J. D. *Kunstreise durch England und Belgien*, Frankfurt a/M., 1833.

PATTISON, MRS. MARK (later LADY DILKE). *The Renaissance of Art in France*, London, 1879. 2 vols. For reference to Foucquet, cf. vol. I, pp. 274-296.

PÈLERIN, JEHAN, called LE VIATEUR. *De artificiali perspectiva*, Toul, 1521.

REINACH, THÉODORE. *Œuvres Complètes de Flavius Josèphe*, *traduites en Français*, Paris, 1900.

RICHTER, L. M. *Chantilly*, London, 1913.

SAINT-RENÉ-TAILLANDIER. 'Un Maître français inconnu.' Article in the *Revue des Deux Mondes*, 1st October, 1865, pp. 796-800.

SPENCER, ELEANOR P. 'Les Heures de Diane de Croy, attribuées à Jehan Fouquet.' Article in the *Gazette des Beaux-Arts*, June 1931, pp. 329-339.

THOMAS, ANTOINE. 'Jacques d'Armagnac Bibliophile.' Article in the *Journal des Savants*, 1906, pp. 633-644.

THOMPSON, HENRY YATES. *Fac-similes of two 'Histoires' by Jean Foucquet from Vols. I and II of the 'Anciennetés des Juifs'*. London, privately printed, 1903.
> *Four photographic fac-similes from detached pages of a fifteenth-century manuscript of 'Histoire Ancienne jusqu'à César' and 'Faits des Romains'*. London, privately printed, 1903.
> 'The Romance of a Book', *Burlington Magazine*, May 1906, pp. 80-84.

THOMPSON, HENRY YATES, and WARNER, GEORGE F. *Miniatures of the School of Fouquet . . . contained in an MS. written about 1475 A.D. for Philippe de Commines, . . .* London, 1907.

THUASNE, L. 'François Fouquet et les Miniatures de la Cité de Dieu de Saint Augustin.' Article in the *Revue des Bibliothèques*, 1898, t. VIII, pp. 33-57.

VALENTINER. *Unknown Masterpieces*, London, 1930.

VALLET DE VIRIVILLE. 'Die Miniaturen des Jehan Fouquet.' Article in the *Athenaeum Français*, November 1855, p. 990.
> 'Jean Fouquet, peintre français du xve siècle.' In the *Revue de Paris*, 1857, August, pp. 409-437; and November, pp. 141-145.
> *Lit de Justice tenu à Vendôme en 1458*. Reprinted in Curmer.

VASARI, GIORGIO. *Le Vite dei piu eccellenti architetti, pittori e scultori*.

VASARI SOCIETY, Vol. IX, p. 25.

Vasnier, H. A. 'L'Architecture dans les œuvres de Memlinc et de Jean Fouquet.' Article in the *Gazette des Beaux-Arts*, 1906, t. I, pp. 195-206.

Viollet, Paul. 'Jehan Foucquet et quelques-uns de ses contemporains.' Article in the *Gazette des Beaux-Arts*, 1867, t. II, pp. 97-113.

Vitry, Paul. 'Zur Ausstellung Französischer Primitiver, einiges über Jean Fouquet und den Meister von Moulins.' Article in the *Zeitschrift für bildende Kunst*, 1904, pp. 290-296.

Waagen, G. F. *Kunstwerke und Künstler in England und Paris.* Berlin, 1837-1839. 3 vols.

Warner, G. F. 'Letter to M. Delisle concerning the ten miniatures of Josephus, Vol. II.' Published in the *Comptes Rendus des Séances de l'Académie des Inscriptions et Belles-Lettres*, 1905, p. 529.

Winkler, Dr. 'Articles in *Zeitschrift für bildende Kunst*: 1919-20, pp. 195-206; 1927-8, pp. 345-349.

INDEX